FROM ROUGH STONES TO WOW

TURN YOUR ROCKS & MINERALS INTO BEAUTIFUL GEMS

JIM MAGNUSON

PUBLICATIONS
Adventure
an imprint of Adventure**KEEN**

To my wife, Diane, for her tireless and patient
support of my passions. She has walked a thousand miles
in my rockhounding and lapidary arts shoes.

From Rough Stones to Wow:
Turn Your Rocks & Minerals into Beautiful Gems

Copyright 2025 by The Magnuson Family Trust
Copyright 2015 by Jim Magnuson and Carol Wood
Originally published as *Gemstone Tumbling, Cutting, Drilling & Cabochon Making*

Cover and book design by Jonathan Norberg
Project editor: Kate Johnson
Proofreader: Emily Beaumont
Indexer: Frances Lennie
Interior and cover photos by Jim Magnuson except where noted on page

Cataloging-in-Publication Data is available from the Library of Congress.
ISBN 978-1-64755-458-3 (pbk.); ISBN 978-1-64755-459-0 (ebook)

Published by Adventure Publications
An imprint of AdventureKEEN
310 Garfield Street South
Cambridge, Minnesota 55008
800-678-7006
adventurepublications.net

SAFETY NOTICE When working with lapidary machines and supplies, it's important to take precautions to avoid a serious health condition known as silicosis, which results from breathing in excessive amounts of rock dust. See page 8 for more details.

CONTENTS

ACKNOWLEDGMENTS

Val Carver Val is the owner and general manager of Minnesota Lapidary Supply and Rocks & Things in Princeton, Minnesota. While he didn't contribute directly to the creation of this edition, many of Val's key insights have been carried forward from the prior edition, and they are critical to the depth and practicality of learning about and practicing lapidary arts. We remain grateful for his contributions to this book and know that he continues to share his knowledge and experience with countless hobbyists and lapidary suppliers.

Richard Paupore Richard is a senior manager at Kingsley North. Located in Norway, Michigan, it is one of the premier makers and sellers of lapidary equipment and supplies in the United States. Richard has a deep knowledge of and passion for the lapidary arts, and he understands and can readily explain the details of a wide range of lapidary equipment and supplies. He is also a skilled practitioner when it comes to using these tools. Finally, he is an excellent photographer and contributed many of the photographs in this book. We appreciate all the time, effort, and experience he contributed, which brought many fresh insights to the second edition, and we are grateful for the contributions his team members made in support of this work.

Wayne Binsfield Wayne is a passionate artist and rockhound who specializes in creating beautiful rock-carving art pieces and other items related to the rockhounding hobby. He runs a small business called Wayne's World Agates and frequents the rock show circuit in the Upper Midwest. Wayne was helpful and generous in sharing his time and talents, which allowed me to create a wonderful new chapter on working with rotary tools, and specifically the sample projects.

Diane Magnuson Diane made a significant contribution by learning about various lapidary processes so she could perform action photography for many detailed activities like cabochon making, drilling, and face-polishing. Additionally, she accompanied me on several rock- and specimen-buying trips to search out and gather high-quality specimens for the gemstone-selection section and for some of the featured lapidary creations.

INTRODUCTION

If you have ever marveled at beautifully cut, polished, and shaped gemstones and wondered what it would take to create your own, you might be surprised at how quickly you can learn how to do it. With a little focused instruction and today's advanced tools and equipment, you can discover the rewarding experience of taking rough stones and making your own creations. And you'll be pleased to learn that creating finished gemstones is quite affordable, especially when compared to many other popular hobbies.

Ten years have passed since the first edition of this book was published. During that time, I've had the opportunity to conduct multiple intensive lapidary workshops with people who were primarily beginners or had just a bit of experience in one or two lapidary skills. While instructing these learners, I used the first edition regularly as an outline and learning aid. This experience gave me insight into ways to adapt and improve the content for a second edition.

Additionally, the outpouring of online feedback has been both overwhelmingly positive and informative as far as suggesting additions or improvements for processes and lapidary machines. I have continued to learn new tips and methods from many practiced lapidary artists who have helped me streamline the learning process and improve the learner's ability to quickly gain confidence and achieve success. Finally, changes in the availability of machines also factored into the need for a second edition. Taken together, our continuous learning and research, along with reader feedback, have resulted not only in a simplification of what we recommended 10 years ago but also in an overall reduction in the startup costs required.

One thing that hasn't changed is the lack of other publications that speak to beginning and intermediate hobbyists about cutting, polishing, and drilling gemstones and making them into cabochons. (These processes are collectively referred to as the lapidary arts.) And while there has been a profusion of videos and informational articles on the internet, this has been accompanied by a significant amount of conflicting and misleading content. Furthermore, there's no cohesion regarding the multiple machines and processes that "play together" and need to work relatively seamlessly to create lapidary products like jewelry pieces.

Another thing that hasn't changed is the desire and need for beginning and intermediate hobbyists to keep things simple: They want to be shown and told what they need to know to perform a given task or activity, without extraneous background information or details. One example of this principle is rock tumbling, to which several publications are solely dedicated. These publications go into depth about the formulation of different tumbling grits, polishing compounds, and tumbling media and are loaded with repetitive information. This might be useful to advanced and specialized tumbling applications, but it goes far beyond the needs or interests of most hobbyists, especially beginners.

With all this in mind, the second edition carries over a large portion of the core material from the first edition. This means we'll provide you with:

1. Recommendations on lapidary machines, including machine types, makes, models, and approximate prices at press time, as well as additional supplies and materials needed.

2. Color photos to illustrate critical processes, supplies, and equipment.

3. Reference charts that help you pull together information on how to go about different projects—starting from the very beginning, with knowing the types of gemstones to use.

4. Simple, easy-to-follow directions that are complemented by action-oriented photos that clearly represent the simplest and most reliable way to perform key operations. Along the way, we show you how a project progresses from raw gemstone to lapidary artwork.

5. Tips, tables, and checklists to jump-start your learning and help you overcome the fear of getting started, stay efficient, and keep costs down. These tools will help beginners achieve success quickly and make the best use of precious time, gemstones, and lapidary supplies. The tables can be used as references for years to come and can be adapted to your own preferences and experiences. Some of the tables provided in the first edition have been significantly streamlined and simplified.

6. Perhaps the most helpful aspect of this book is that, in addition to covering lapidary processes and the equipment necessary to perform them, we show how these techniques and tools relate to each other and how they work together to take you from start to finish.

Based on the insights mentioned above, this edition contains significant new content and major revisions. Many changes are specifically targeted to address learner and reader feedback and to ensure we are providing the most current and valuable information available. Notably, the second edition incorporates these major changes:

1. Discussion of vertical-wheel, or vertical-arbor, grinding-and-polishing machines (cabbers) in addition to the flat lapidary grinder-polishers (flat laps) discussed in the prior edition.

2. Addition of a chapter on working with rotary hand tools, such as Dremels.

3. Recommendation of alternative tumblers for both rotary and vibratory tumbling, including a beginner's vibratory tumbler that can do coarse-grinding of rough stones.

4. Removal of the routing chapter because it has proven to be less valuable than other content and because there are many better alternatives to creating pendant necklaces.

5. Removal of the dopping process and machine because there is a much simpler and cheaper method.

6. Rewrite of the jewelry-making chapter to focus on simpler methods and types of jewelry, such as the use of glue-on bails, pinch bails, and preformed bezel cups. All the featured jewelry projects will be achievable by beginners.

As with the first edition, our goal with this book is to provide a one-stop shop for beginners and others who have recently started their lapidary journey. Some of you may have tried out a lapidary process, such as tumbling, only to get frustrated and quit altogether. We'll help you avoid that. We have intentionally left out the most complex and costly lapidary methods and machines, such as commercial equipment and "combination machines" (arbor–trim saw combinations, for example). Specifically, we exclude more advanced skills like silversmithing, making spheres or marbles, and faceting, all of which are better suited to more-focused instructional guides and hands-on training.

Instead, this book keeps it simple and covers a variety of the most popular lapidary arts, helping you produce high-quality gemstone products that you will be proud to display, wear, or even sell.

We'd like to leave you with one last tip, and that is to always put progress before perfection. Your first tries are just that; take a moment to review the processes and reflect on what you might do differently on your next activity. I like to think I've mastered all of the processes in this book, but I'm still learning and adapting, and that's what keeps me coming back for more!

CHAPTER 1:
GETTING STARTED

In this chapter, we'll cover the basics of gemstone materials, the types of lapidary products you can make from them, and the general processes and lapidary machines you need to know about.

Most hobbyists start with the simplest projects and work their way up; others have a specific goal in mind, like making jewelry, and therefore want to quickly learn each of the necessary operations. Regardless of where you fall on this spectrum, keep in mind that lapidary supply stores can provide you with gemstones that have been partially processed (such as crushed rocks for tumbling or slabs for trimming and making jewelry pieces), which allows you to jump in wherever you are comfortable or most interested.

GEMSTONE MATERIALS COMMONLY USED IN LAPIDARY WORK

Not all stones are suitable for performing lapidary arts, and there are some that are quite difficult to work with, so in this book we focus on a variety of accessible and affordable stones that you can turn into beautiful showpieces and jewelry. Furthermore, we prioritize some of the more popular gems and minerals currently sought after and used by both beginner and professional lapidarists. To work a stone, it must be hard enough to be cut, shaped, and polished. The Mohs hardness scale is used to express the hardness of minerals, with a hardness of 1 being the softest (talc has a hardness of 1) and 10 being the hardest (diamonds are a 10). The majority of stones that we recommend are in the 6–7 range; examples include agate, jasper, labradorite, and tiger's-eye. There is an endless variety of colors and patterns in the gemstones we recommend, so they will be suitable for whatever project you want to complete. On occasion, these gemstones differ in hardness; when this affects a lapidary process, we'll give you tips on how to work such a stone.

In addition to selecting the types of gemstones that you want to use, take the time to choose stones with pleasing colors and patterns. The saying "Garbage in, garbage out" is nowhere more true than in the lapidary arts—in fact, we have adapted the saying specifically to lapidary work: "Garbage in, shiny garbage out." All of your fine work cutting and polishing will be wasted on poor-quality stones. This doesn't mean that you need to spend a fortune on acquiring expensive raw materials; the types of stones we recommend can be obtained at reasonable prices, and you can even find them on your own rockhounding adventures. That being said, if you are just a beginner, it's perfectly acceptable, and in fact advisable, to use (and learn on) lower-quality stones.

PRODUCTS YOU CAN MAKE WITH YOUR GEMSTONE MATERIALS

Once you have selected a few stones you'd like to work with, it's time to decide what to do with them. There are many ways to use your gemstones. You can polish the whole stones in a tumbler, you can polish just a portion of the stone (its face), or you can prepare your gemstones for use in jewelry. If you're planning on using them in jewelry, you can use the whole stones in one piece; slice them and use sections in your jewelry pieces; or use them to create a cabochon, which is a shaped, domed, and polished stone commonly used in jewelry. Below are some examples of the lapidary products we'll be teaching you how to make, with reference to the lapidary processes used to make them.

Tumble-polished whole stones for display. These stones have been fully polished on all sides and are usually displayed in glass bowls and jars as eye candy.

Tumble-polished whole stones for use in jewelry. These stones are face-drilled (drilled through from front to back) or top-drilled (drilled into the top), with the holes used to attach a jewelry finding; they can also be wire wrapped.

Natural-shape cut-stone pendants for use in jewelry. Whole gemstones have been cut into slabs and left in the natural shape of a whole stone, such as an agate. The pendants are tumble-polished and then wrapped with copper, bronze, silver, or gold wire; wrapping designs can range from simple to elaborate. Pendants can also be either face-drilled or top-drilled, with the holes used to attach a jewelry finding.

Cabochon pendants for use in jewelry. These stones have been cut into thin slabs or slices, then shaped into ovals, circles, squares, or other shapes and placed into a jewelry setting. Cabochons can be face-drilled or top-drilled, with the holes used to attach a jewelry finding. You can also attach a glue-on bail, or the pieces can be wire wrapped or set in a bezel cup.

Face-polished or dome-polished stones. The most beautiful face of a whole stone (for example, an agate) is polished, showcasing the color and pattern on the polished face and the natural formation of the rough, unfinished sides.

Stone carvings. Whole stones or cabochons can be used for stone carvings. The simplest designs are two-dimensional on soft stones like basalt; complex pieces are three-dimensional and incorporate the existing pattern on gemstones like agates.

LAPIDARY MACHINES

To create the lapidary products we discuss, you will need specific lapidary machines, tools, and supplies. Because this book is about demystifying the process for beginners, we will provide detailed information about machinery and specific recommendations to get you started quickly. Note that all the machines we recommend in this book are made specifically for lapidary work. Many people attempt to adapt things like tile saws or drills for woodworking, but many of these are unsafe for lapidary work and don't produce satisfactory results.

MACHINE DEFINITIONS AND USES

Safety note: Before providing details about lapidary machines and supplies, we'd like to provide a general safety recommendation about a serious health condition known as silicosis, which results from inhaling excessive amounts of rock dust. Using lubricants (water or rockhound oil) when cutting and grinding gemstones is the best way to minimize your chances of developing this condition. Therefore, all the machines and processes we'll cover in this book ensure that more than 90% of rock dust is captured by the given lubricants. To provide additional safety, we also recommend having a good ventilating fan in your work area, and you can use a respirator or an N95 or KN95 mask to further reduce the possibility of inhaling rock dust. These latter precautions are especially important when you are doing a lot of coarse-grinding or working with more-toxic materials, such as malachite and tiger's-eye (for a comprehensive list, see the International Gem Society's Gemstone Toxicity Table at gemsociety.org /article/gemstone-toxicity-table).

- **Tumblers** are enclosed, hardened-rubber barrels that either rotate (rotary tumblers) or vibrate (vibratory tumblers) to gradually smooth and polish your gemstones.

- **Lapidary drill presses** are similar to drill presses made for drilling into metal or wood, but they operate at lower speeds and require water or other cooling fluids to reduce heat buildup on the drill bits; drill presses can be used either to drill all the way through a stone (face-drilling) or into the top of a stone (top-drilling).

- **Trim saws** are primarily used to cut away excess material from precut slabs, and most of these have a 6-inch blade. They have smaller motors and generally are unable to cut stones much larger than 1 inch in diameter, especially very hard stones like agates, which are rated a 7 on the Mohs hardness scale.

- **Slab saws** are all-purpose lapidary saws for cutting slabs out of rough rocks; cutting away broken and chipped faces of gemstones (so they can be face-polished); or trimming excess material, as with trim saws. For most hobbyists, a slab saw with a 10-inch blade is sufficient in terms of both size and power.

- **Flat lapidary grinders and polishers (flat laps)** are used to create cabochons and to shape and polish one side, or face, of a whole stone using a series of coarse- to fine-mesh discs and a polishing disc.

- **Cabbers** perform the same functions as flat laps, except vertical wheels are used instead of horizontal discs.

WHAT LAPIDARY MACHINES WILL I NEED?

IF YOU WANT TO MAKE	YOU WILL NEED
Tumble-polished whole stones	Rotary or vibratory tumbler (note that most vibratory tumblers can't perform the coarse-grinding stage of tumbling; only the Raytech TV-5 can do this part of the process)
Tumble-polished whole stones used in jewelry	Rotary or vibratory tumbler and lapidary drill press (a drill press isn't needed if stones will be wire wrapped)
Natural-shape cut-stone pendants used in jewelry	Rotary or vibratory tumbler, rock saw, and lapidary drill press (a drill press isn't needed if stones will be wire wrapped or used with a glue-on pendant bail)
Cabochons or shaped stone pendants used in jewelry	Rotary or vibratory tumbler, rock saw, flat lap grinder-polisher, and lapidary drill press (a drill press isn't needed if stones will be wire wrapped; placed in a jewelry setting, such as a bezel cup; or used with a glue-on pendant bail). *For cabochons:* A tumbler is optional for finishing pieces; a cabber can be used instead of a flat-lap (i.e. one or the other).
Face- or dome-polished stones	Flat lap grinder-polisher and (optional) rock saw. *For face-polishing:* A cabber can be used instead of a flat lap (i.e. one or the other).

LAPIDARY MACHINE AND SUPPLY PRICING

Listed below are 2024 prices for some of the lapidary equipment and supplies needed to perform each lapidary process. Because there has been so much change and turnover in the lapidary machine business, we felt it was critical to provide both a top recommendation and some honorable mentions. *However, rest assured that all of these machines have been proven to deliver years of reliable service without needing to replace custom parts.* Prices are representative of what you might find at a full-service lapidary supply store, and they will of course vary over time.

LAPIDARY SUPPLIES LIST

░ Top Recommendation ░ Honorable Mention

ITEM	PRICE

Tumbling

ITEM	PRICE
Lortone 3-lb. rotary tumbler	$125
Central Machinery double 3-lb. barrel rotary tumbler	$70
Thumler's Tumbler AR-2 double 3-lb. barrel rotary tumbler	$225
Diamond Pacific Mini-Sonic MT-4 4-lb. vibratory tumbler	$450
Raytech TV-5 vibratory tumbler (double-barrel kit)	$178
Lot-O-Tumbler vibratory tumbler	$305
GemOro Sparkle Spa	$50
EuroSonic ultrasonic cleaning solution for GemOro Sparkle Spa (8 oz.)	$4
Coarse tumbling grit (60–90 mesh; 1 lb.)	$4
Medium tumbling grit (120–220 mesh; 1 lb.)	$4
Fine tumbling grit (600 mesh; 1 lb.)	$5
Micro alumina polish (1 lb.)	$8
Large ceramic media (1 lb.)	$5
Small ceramic media (1 lb.)	$9

Cutting

ITEM	PRICE
Hi-Tech Diamond 6" trim-only saw	$480
Johnson Brothers Rock Rascal Model J Complete 6" rock-cutting and trim saw	$430
Covington Engineering 6" rock-cutting and trim saw	$530
Kingsley North LTS6 6" rock-cutting and trim saw	$636
Hi-Tech Diamond 10" rock-cutting and trim saw	$850
Lortone 10" rock-cutting and trim saw	$810
6" saw blade (6" x .032" x ⅝")	$45
10" saw blade (10" x .032" x ⅝")	$65
Rockhound oil (1 gal.)	$25

Cabochon Making and Face-Polishing

Hi-Tech Diamond All-U-Need 8" flat or slant lapidary grinder-polisher with accessory kit	$650
Ameritool Universal 8" flat lapidary grinder-polisher with accessory kit	$695
Kingsley North KNC6 6" cabber	$1,400
CabKing 6V3 6" cabber	$1,400
8" flat lap replacement disc (100 and 180 mesh)	$30
8" flat lap replacement disc (325, 600, and 1200 mesh)	$36
8" flat lap replacement disc-polishing felt pad	$10
8" flat lap cerium-charged polishing disc	$45
Polishing paste (14,000 mesh; 10 g)	$15
6" replacement wheel for Kingsley North KNC6 and CabKing 6V3 (80, 100, and 220 mesh)	$85
6" replacement wheel for Kingsley North KNC6 and CabKing 6V3 (280, 600, 1,200, and 3,000 mesh)	$56

Drilling

EuroTool benchtop drill press	$105
Micro-Mark MicroLux 3-speed drill press	$180
Drill bits (1.5 mm, 2 mm, or 2.5 mm; 20 count; such as Drilax)	$20
Adjustable mini vise (from Minnesota Lapidary Supply)	$28
Zona 37-200 mini vise	$32

Rotary Hand Tool Applications

Dremel 3000-1/24	$75
Dremel flex-shaft tool, hanger, and compatible foot pedal (for carving)	$71
Dremel drill press workstation	$50
Foredom K.2230 with hanger and foot pedal (for advanced carving)	$442
Dremel-compatible 50-piece diamond burr set (such as Luo ke)	$15
Rocaris 40-pack 1" abrasive buffing wheel set for rotary tool (10 pieces each of 120, 180, 320, and 400 grit)	$10
Dremel 726-01 20-piece cleaning/polishing accessory kit	$15
Drilax 50-Piece diamond drill bit and burr set	$25
Tabletop swivel vise with rubber jaws	$20
Water pump and drip system	$50
Zam buffing and polishing compound (¼ lb.)	$6

OTHER USEFUL SUPPLIES

These supplies aren't specific to the lapidary hobby but are useful for multiple lapidary processes covered in this book. We won't list them in each chapter.

- **Sound-blocking headphones** or foam earplugs

- **Protective eyewear,** such as goggles or safety glasses

- **N95 or KN95 masks** (or a respirator if you have breathing sensitivities or will be working with toxic materials)

- **Trays and storage units** for sorting and storing materials

- **5-gallon buckets** for emptying out water containing grit or rock dust

- **Plastic colander with handles** that can be set over the 5-gallon buckets

- **Water jugs** for refilling water-supply cups and reservoirs

- **Durable tarps and indoor-outdoor carpet mats** to protect your walls and floors from oil and water spray; you can also temporarily hang painting tarps from the ceiling to contain water and oil spray within a more localized area

- **Shop rags and old towels**

- **Adjustable desk lamps**

- **Lighted magnifying glass**

- **Degreasing dishwashing liquid** (such as Dawn or Ajax)

- **Spray bottle**

- **Scrub brush**

- **Inexpensive plastic 2-oz. medicine cups** for measuring grits (one for each type of grit or polish compound you'll be using)

- **Fine-point permanent marker** (such as Sharpie)

- **Regular graphite pencil**

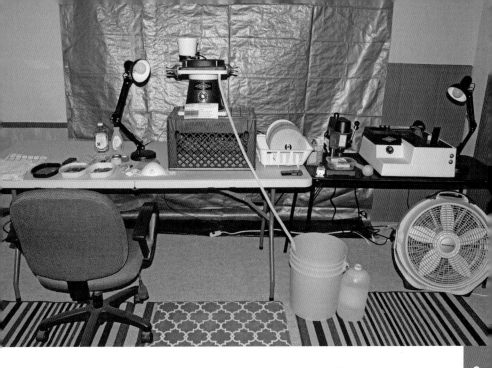

WORKSHOP SETUP AND OPERATION

A major consideration for lapidary hobbyists is designating and setting up a workspace that is suitable for working with various machines and materials. Some of the aspects to be considered include the following.

- **Noise** is a major consideration when operating saws, grinding-and-polishing machines, and even rock tumblers (especially vibratory tumblers like the Raytech TV-5). Operating your equipment in a remote basement area, garage, or shed is a great way to help you keep peace with your family (and the neighbors).

- **Cleanliness** is also an issue in your workspace. Consider using canvas painters' dropcloths or plastic tarps to contain the fine mist or spray that will be escaping into the air around saws, drills, and grinding-and-polishing machines. You'll also want to cover the floor in your work area and any nearby items you want to protect. This is especially important when using oil-based lubricants for your saw.

- **Organization** will make you more efficient, keep things contained in a designated area, and help you keep track of what needs to be restocked. Consider getting some shelving units and adding labels for the supplies and materials that will be kept there. Bench tables are great for tasks like stenciling gemstone slabs, making jewelry, and cleaning materials between tasks. Ergonomic and sturdy workbenches are critical when

13

you're spending considerable time performing various tasks like sawing, grinding, and polishing.

- **Lighting and ventilation** are especially important in lapidary work. Start with an area that has good airflow and lighting, and supplement with fans and directional lighting as needed.

FURTHER INSTRUCTION

Get acquainted with a well-established lapidary supply shop. If you're lucky, there will be one within driving distance that you can visit in person (otherwise, you should find one online and establish a relationship). Many jewelry and beading stores offer classes on jewelry making that may include instruction in the related lapidary processes. While you may be able to save money by shopping online for the lowest price on a given piece of equipment, you will be glad to have the advice of an expert when something isn't going as expected or a machine isn't functioning properly, and it's nice to get tips on new tools, processes, and supplies. Some shops even create specially adapted equipment that will streamline or simplify processes even more than we describe in this book. Through this relationship, you will probably also get to know other amateur lapidary artists in your area that you can share your ideas and creations with.

We also urge you to find a local rock and mineral club and join it. Every club has a few true lapidary artists, and almost invariably they will generously offer their time and patient advice. Getting hands-on practice with someone who has learned the tricks of the trade is invaluable. These lapidary veterans may also show you other methods that better suit your personal style. So join a club and find a comfortable place to learn and, as you improve, to share your own skills.

And when it comes to lapidary work, one last thing to keep in mind is that everyone has their own personal style and preferences. As your skills improve, your interests will grow and evolve as you are introduced to the incredibly diverse world of cutting, polishing, and jewelry making. As we like to say: Learn, adapt, create!

HELPFUL TIP If you become a regular customer at a lapidary supply store or join a local rock club, you might be able to get a discount; it never hurts to ask.

CHAPTER 2:
CHOOSING GEMSTONES

GEMSTONE TYPES AND LAPIDARY USES

Now that you've gotten a general introduction to the type of gemstone material best suited for beginner and intermediate lapidary hobbyists and artists, we'll show you which gemstones are best for specific types of lapidary work.

Not all gemstones can be used in the same way. For example, some gemstones are too large to be tumble-polished or face-polished as individual stones. If you want to polish such specimens, they must first be cut into slabs and then shaped into jewelry pieces. The table on pages 18–19 provides a guide to the uses each gemstone is best suited for. While this table is by no means exhaustive, the materials we recommend provide a broad cross section of what is readily available and affordable and will enable beginner and intermediate lapidary artists to produce outstanding finished stones and jewelry pieces.

GEMSTONE PRICES

Most of the stones we recommend in this book can be purchased in bulk and are priced by the pound. The low end of the price range is about $3–$5 per pound; medium-level stones are $8–$15 per pound; and high-priced stones go for more than $20 per pound. As you gain skill and confidence, you may choose stones on the higher end of the range, but you can produce many delightful lapidary products with carefully selected gemstones from the low end as well.

SELECTING HIGH-QUALITY GEMSTONES

Once you know which gemstone you want to use and how you want to use it, you'll need to be able to recognize high-quality specimens to purchase. Just as choosing lousy produce at the grocery store will get you a subpar dinner, lower-quality stones will lead to less than optimal results: Garbage in, shiny garbage out. While it will certainly take time for you to consistently achieve high-quality results, starting with high-quality stones is the best way to avoid frustration.

GEMSTONES AT A GLANCE

TYPE	COST	MOHS HARDNESS RATING	USES			
			Tumble-Polishing	Face-Polishing	Natural-Shape Cabochon	Shaped Cabochon
Amethyst Quartz	$–$$	6	Yes	No	No	Yes
Bahia Agate	$–$$	7	Yes	Yes	Yes	Yes
Biggs Jasper	$–$$	7	Yes	No	No	Yes
Blue Lace Agate	$$	7	Yes	Yes	Yes	Yes
Botswana Agate	$–$$	7	Yes	Yes	Yes	Yes
Brazilian Agate	$–$$	7	Yes	Yes	Yes	Yes
Carnelian Agate	$–$$	7	Yes	Yes	Yes	Yes
Chevron Amethyst	$–$$	7	Yes	No	No	Yes
Crazy Lace Agate	$–$$	6	No	Yes	No	Yes
Emberlite (Fluorescent Sodalite)	$–$$	5	Yes	No	No	Yes
Labradorite	$–$$	7	Yes	Yes	No	Yes
Laguna Agate	$$–$$$	7	No	Yes	Yes	Yes
Lake Superior Agate	$$–$$$	7	Yes	Yes	Yes	Yes
Lapis Lazuli	$$–$$$	5	Yes	No	No	Yes
Leopard Skin Jasper	$–$$	6	Yes	No	No	Yes
Malawi Agate	$$–$$$	7	No	Yes	Yes	Yes

HELPFUL TIP When we recommend against using a specific type of stone for a given project, it doesn't necessarily mean it can't be used. In some cases it can work, but it will likely take some additional effort and may not be the best use for the given type of stone.

TYPE	COST	MOHS HARDNESS RATING	USES			
			Tumble-Polishing	Face-Polishing	Natural-Shape Cabochon	Shaped Cabochon
Montana Moss Agate	$–$$	7	No	Yes	No	Yes
Mookaite Jasper	$$	7	Yes	No	No	Yes
Moonstone	$$–$$$	7	No	No	Yes	Yes
Obsidian (Multiple Varieties)	$	6	Yes	No	No	Yes
Ocean Jasper	$$–$$$	6	Yes	No	No	Yes
Petrified Wood (Multiple Varieties)	$–$$	7	Yes	Yes	No	Yes
Picture Jasper	$$–$$$	7	Yes	No	No	Yes
Rhodonite	$$	6	Yes	No	No	Yes
Rose Quartz	$–$$	6	Yes	No	No	Yes
Sodalite	$–$$	6	Yes	No	No	Yes
Teepee Canyon and Fairburn Agates	$$–$$$	7	Yes	Yes	Yes	Yes
Tiger's-Eye	$–$$	6	Yes	No	No	Yes

$ = $3–$5 per pound $$ = $8–$15 per pound $$$ = over $20 per pound

HELPFUL TIP In some cases, higher-grade stones are available, but they can be expensive; if you're a beginner, these are not your best bet, as there is more to lose if you accidentally damage them. For the sake of learning new processes and equipment, it's actually best to start with low-grade materials.

A VISUAL GUIDE TO SELECTING GEMSTONES

To give you an idea of where to start, we've selected 12 gemstones from the table on the previous pages to discuss in further detail. These are good stand-ins for a number of others in the table, and the same selection tips apply to them as well. To make things as intuitive as possible, on the following pages we've provided photos for each gemstone showing rough stones that are below lapidary grade, rough stones that we consider lapidary grade, cut slabs, and at least one completed lapidary piece, or cabochon, ready for jewelry making. This combination of images will help demystify this part of the process and help you select high-quality materials.

As their name suggests, **below-grade** stones don't warrant the effort and cost necessary for them to serve as display stones or jewelry pieces (though they are great for learning). In contrast, **lapidary-grade** (medium- and high-grade) stones represent the sweet spot for most of your lapidary products; these stones would make nice jewelry pieces or tumble-polished stones for display. For stones that contain patterns or banding (such as agates, jaspers, or petrified wood), the primary characteristics you're looking for are brightness and intensity of color, color separation (including distinctive layering or banding patterns), and unique coloration. When it comes to non-patterned and monotone materials (quartz varieties, black obsidian, aventurine), lower-quality stones are milkier or dull in color, while higher-quality stones are purer, less fractured, and brightly or uniquely colored.

Rather than listing similar types of gemstones for each of the example stones pictured below, we've included the following criteria as a guide. Keep in mind that there are variations in hardness within these groupings, which is an important consideration for things like tumbling where you might want to mix different types of stones. More details are provided throughout the book.

1. Most agates share the same selection and processing criteria: brightness, intensity of color and pattern, and hardness.

2. Most jaspers and petrified wood types share the same selection and processing criteria: brightness, intensity of color and pattern, and hardness.

3. Quartz-based stones can be grouped with an additional criteria of clarity.

4. Obsidian, sodalite, rhodonite, tiger's-eye, and lapis lazuli share the same selection and processing criteria.

BOTSWANA AGATE

A rough-cut slab (above right) and a few nicely finished cabochons (above left). If you use small, whole stones, you can create pendants with unique natural shapes.

Medium-grade (above left) and high-grade (above right) stones show nice color variations and distinctive, high-contrast patterns.

Below-grade stones show almost no visible pattern, sometimes with a lot of quartz fill. Note, however, that Botswana agates sometimes require an exploratory cut to determine whether the banding patterns and colors are of lapidary quality.

21

CHEVRON AMETHYST

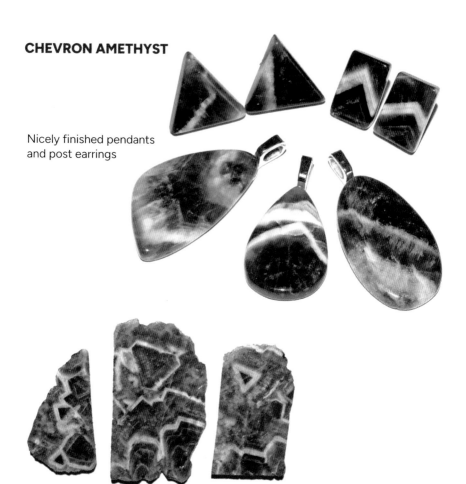

Nicely finished pendants and post earrings

A rough-cut slab

Medium-grade (right) and high-grade (far right) stones have rich, vibrant colors with some chevron patterning.

Below-grade stones have dull and washed-out colors with non-distinctive patterning.

CRAZY LACE AGATE

Some beautiful cabochons

Here you can see both sides of a slab with excellent banding plus crazy lace agate's signature patterns and colors. When deciding how to use this gemstone for lapidary work, you will have lots of options for where to mark your stencil lines and saw cuts.

Medium-grade (below right) and high-grade (right and far right) specimens have superb and finely detailed banding patterns; once the stones have been cut into slabs, they will offer several nice options for cabochon shapes.

Below-grade specimens have very little banding pattern visible on the exterior, though it's usually worth cutting a stone in half to see if there is more pattern on the interior.

23

LABRADORITE

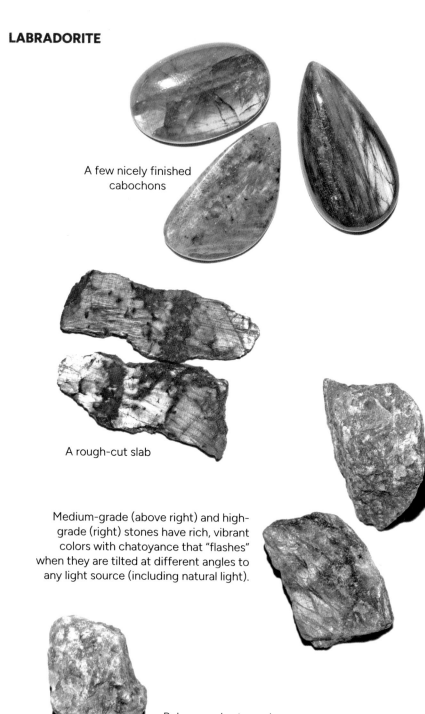

A few nicely finished cabochons

A rough-cut slab

Medium-grade (above right) and high-grade (right) stones have rich, vibrant colors with chatoyance that "flashes" when they are tilted at different angles to any light source (including natural light).

Below-grade stones have minimal or no visible chatoyance or are heavily fractured.

LAKE SUPERIOR AGATE

Cut slabs (right) and jewelry pieces (below) using cabochons and a polished natural-shape slab. If you use small, whole stones, the finished products have unique natural shapes.

CHOOSING GEMSTONES

High-grade (right) and medium-grade (above) specimens show nice color variations and some banding patterns.

Below-grade specimens show almost no visible pattern. Note, however, that Lake Superior agates sometimes require an exploratory cut to determine whether the banding patterns and colors are of lapidary quality. Above (in center of page) you can see a medium-grade stone that has been cut to show beautiful interior colors and pattern.

25

LAPIS LAZULI

Jewelry pieces using cabochons set in 925 silver (sterling silver) settings

Slabs have a striking deep-blue-and-white color scheme with flecks of pyrite that will yield the shimmering qualities for which this gemstone is prized. When using it for cabochons, you can achieve a range of colors.

Medium-grade (above left and center) and high-grade (above right) stones have both a deep-blue coloration and the prized gold-colored matrix. The gold coloration occurs because of pyrite mineral inclusions and impurities.

Below-grade stones have material with a chalky-white matrix, and they lack the striking deep-blue coloration found in higher-quality gemstone material.

LEOPARD SKIN JASPER

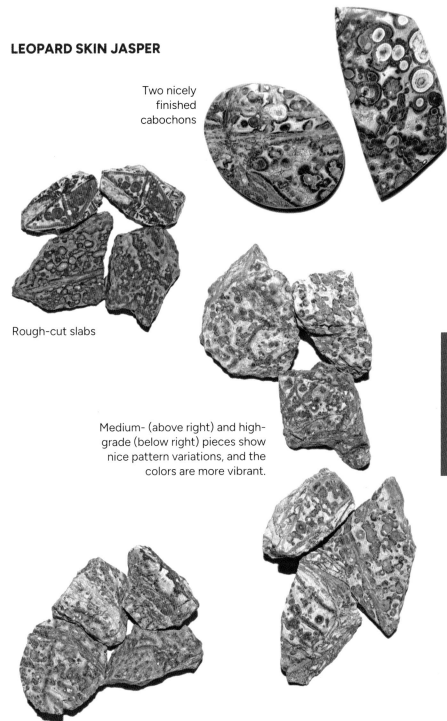

Two nicely finished cabochons

Rough-cut slabs

Medium- (above right) and high-grade (below right) pieces show nice pattern variations, and the colors are more vibrant.

Below-grade specimens show almost no visible pattern, with dull or muddy colors.

MOOKAITE JASPER

A nicely finished cabochon

Rough-cut slabs

Medium-grade (above left) and high-grade (above right) pieces show a rich array of vibrant colors.

Below-grade specimens have minimal or very monochrome colors.

OBSIDIAN (MAHOGANY AND SNOWFLAKE VARIETIES)

Cut slabs (left and above left) make for beautiful jewelry pieces, such as the cabochons shown above.

Medium-grade (above left) and high-grade (above right) specimens are glassy and show hints of nice color variations that may be revealed when cut into slabs. Like some other gemstones, you will discover more about the quality of the stone as you cut into successive layers.

Below-grade stones lack the color variability and inclusions found in higher-quality materials.

PETRIFIED WOOD

A bright and colorful petrified wood cabochon

This slab is incredibly intense, and there are numerous sections that would lend well to cutting, either using a stencil or creating free-form shapes.

Medium-grade (above left) and high-grade (above center and right) petrified wood exhibits the characteristic wood-grain pattern, and these specimens from Arizona have gorgeous rainbow colors. Even if a stone shows wood-grain patterning, making an exploratory cut is often worthwhile, as it allows you to see if the interior pattern is better suited for tumble-polishing or cabochons.

Below-grade petrified wood is often a dull gray or brown; while such specimens are still interesting, they are probably best suited for a rock garden, aquarium, or similar type of display. Just as with agates and jaspers, innumerable varieties of petrified wood are found around the world.

TEEPEE CANYON AND FAIRBURN AGATES

Two exciting new gemstone types featured in this edition are the closely related Teepee Canyon and Fairburn agates, both found in the Black Hills of South Dakota. These agates can also be found as fully exposed and naturally tumbled specimens in the prairies and grasslands east of the Black Hills, but those agates are so rare and valuable that it's usually impractical to use them for jewelry. Rough rock specimens that have been mined out of the Black Hills are equally beautiful and can yield high-grade material for lapidary work.

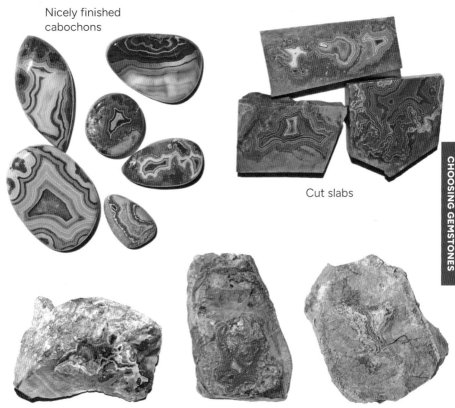

Nicely finished cabochons

Cut slabs

CHOOSING GEMSTONES

Medium-grade (above left) and high-grade (above center and right) specimens show nice color variations and some banding patterns.

Below-grade specimens show almost no visible pattern. Note, however, that most come from within the Black Hills and are embedded in host-rock nodules that require substantial cutting and trimming. As you cut away the rough material, you are able to determine whether the banding patterns and colors are of lapidary quality.

TIGER'S-EYE

The cabochons are first-class, with striking color variations and iridescence. To see the full beauty of tiger's-eye, you'll need to tilt it at different angles in both natural and artificial light.

These precut slabs show off the beautiful iridescence and banding layers that make tiger's-eye famous. Tiger's-eye comes in three different color shades, gold, blue, and red.

Medium-grade (right and far right) and high-grade (below right) specimens a beautiful section of tiger's-eye pattern. Replete with striking lines and bright colors, they will almost certainly yield high-quality slabs. However, when it comes to tiger's-eye, we recommend that beginners buy precut slabs that show contrasting color bands. It takes time to learn how to cut tiger's-eye to produce the best lapidary specimens.

Below-grade tiger's-eye has minimal iridescence and less well-defined bands than higher-grade stones.

CHOOSING GEMSTONES

CHAPTER 3:
TUMBLE-POLISHING

OVERVIEW

Tumble-polishing refers to gently rolling or vibrating gemstones, along with tumbling media and grinding or polishing compounds, in a tumbler barrel (drum) until the stones reach a matte, semigloss, or high-gloss finish. It is a relatively straightforward, repetitive process that progresses through multiple cycles. Thorough and patient cleaning of the stones between cycles is the best recipe for success.

LAPIDARY EQUIPMENT AND SUPPLIES NEEDED

Tumbling requires a rock tumbler. There are two primary options: **Rotary tumblers** are best for removing jagged edges and producing more rounded stones, but they take up to six times longer than a vibratory tumbler. **Vibratory tumblers** are fast, efficient, and gentler on your stones, but they make considerably more noise and need more regular attention. From a practical standpoint, all vibratory tumblers (other than the **Raytech TV-5**) are primarily used for finishing jewelry pieces or cabochons because of their inability to coarse-grind rough stones. Both types of machines use silicon carbide abrasives (grits) for grinding and aluminum oxide polishing compounds.

TIME REQUIREMENTS

Rotary tumbling takes 40 days from rough stones to a high-gloss polish. Most vibratory tumblers take six days for a high-gloss finish, but you need to start with stones or cabochon pieces that are partially tumbled or sanded with either a flat lapidary grinder or a cabber machine. The Raytech TV-5 vibratory tumbler takes 14 days from rough stones to a high-gloss polish.

RECOMMENDED EQUIPMENT AND SUPPLIES

ROTARY TUMBLERS

Lortone 3-A single-barrel rotary tumbler   RICHARD PAUPORE

Thumler's Tumbler 15-pound Model B rotary tumbler   RICHARD PAUPORE

Central Machinery double-barrel rotary tumbler

There are likely more than 100 makes, models, sizes, and types of tumblers. We are going to focus on only a few of these because they have been proven the world over to be the machines of choice for amateur lapidary artists. While these are not the only machines that can produce high-quality results, they are both affordable and reliable, so they will provide many years of use and enjoyment. We also want to reiterate here that machines that are lower in price and quality are often a recipe for frustration and can lead you to give up on tumble-polishing gemstones.

Regardless of which make or model you purchase, we recommend a hardened-rubber barrel (drum). This is not only because a rubber barrel is noise dampening but also because a plastic barrel will become coated/contaminated with abrasives, resulting in poor-quality polishing results. Our top recommendation for 3-pound rotary tumblers is twofold: First is the Lortone 3-A single-barrel tumbler, and second is the Central Machinery double-barrel tumbler (both are pictured above). Our secondary recommendation for 3-pound-capacity tumblers is the Thumler's Tumbler AR-2 double-barrel tumbler (not shown). For the larger (12- to 17-pound-capacity) rotary tumblers, our top recommendation is the Thumler's Tumbler 15-pound Model B (pictured above), and our secondary recommendation is the Rebel 17-pound tumbler.

A couple of widely sold rotary tumblers that we *cannot* recommend are the National Geographic and Tumble-Bee brands. Both machines have a number of reported issues with quality and reliability, and the National Geographic tumbler only has a 2-pound capacity.

VIBRATORY TUMBLERS

Raytech TV-5 4-pound vibratory full-service tumbler

Diamond Pacific Mini-Sonic MT-4 4-pound vibratory finishing tumbler
RICHARD PAUPORE

TUMBLE-POLISHING

Vibratory tumblers are considerably more expensive than rotary tumblers, but because they are primarily used for finishing jewelry pieces, you don't need a large-capacity machine. We recommend Diamond Pacific's Mini-Sonic MT-4 machine for its durability, reliability, and high-quality construction with a hard rubber barrel. Our secondary recommendation is the Lot-O-Tumbler, which is also a durable and high-quality machine.

The Raytech TV-5 is the only full-service vibratory tumbler for both coarse-grinding and finishing of stones and jewelry pieces, and it's less than half the cost of most vibratory tumblers, so it's our primary recommendation for a full-service tumbler and our secondary recommendation if you intend to use it primarily for finishing jewelry pieces. The TV-5 has all the advantages of regular vibratory tumblers, though it's not quite as gentle on stones or jewelry pieces because the barrel is hard plastic instead of rubber (which also means it's considerably noisier). Additional advantages are that it can perform coarse-grinding for rough stones, and it's about half the price of other vibratory tumblers. Also, because the lid is clear, you can see the stones moving inside, which is especially exciting for young hobbyists, and you can see whether you're getting the right motion inside the barrel. Finally, the more hands-on process keeps you more engaged during each tumbling stage.

Note: If you have both a rotary and a vibratory tumbler, you can use the rotary tumbler for coarse-grinding and then perform medium- and fine-grinding and polishing in your vibratory tumbler.

TUMBLERS COMPARED

ROTARY TUMBLER ADVANTAGES	VIBRATORY TUMBLER ADVANTAGES	TV-5 VIBRATORY TUMBLER ADVANTAGES
Quieter; sounds almost like a small brook, with water running over the stones in the streambed	Five times faster for finishing jewelry pieces starting with the medium-grit stage (6 days on average for vibratory vs. 30 days on average for rotary)	All the advantages of regular vibratory tumblers (though it's not as quiet or as gentle on stones because it has a hard plastic barrel instead of rubber)
Cheaper initial cost ($125 for a small rotary vs. $330 for a small vibratory)	Uses one-third to half the amount of abrasive and polishing compound per load vs. rotary tumblers, offsetting the higher purchase price	At $180, it's about half the price of other vibratory tumblers and in the middle of the rotary tumbler cost range
Removes more stone when needed, such as with rough stones or stones that you want to be more rounded	Less fracturing of stones, which is critical for softer stones and jewelry pendant slabs and cabs	Can perform coarse-grinding for rough stones
Less maintenance; you can turn it on and walk away for 10 days per tumbling stage	Top loading allows for inspection of stones and slurry as they process and allows you to add water on the fly	
	Top loading makes for easier cleanup; just add soap and water at the end of each stage, then empty the tumbler barrel into a bucket	

HELPFUL TIP If you decide to go with one of each tumbler type, you should consider getting a large (12- to 17-pound-capacity) rotary tumbler and a small vibratory tumbler. The small vibratory tumbler will keep up with the larger rotary tumbler. In a two-machine setup, you'll do coarse-grit, or rough, tumbling in the rotary tumbler to shape or round out the stones, and then do the medium-grit, fine-grit, and polishing steps in the vibratory tumbler.

TUMBLING SUPPLIES

Abrasives: (from left to right) coarse, medium, and fine grits and polishing compound with plastic containers and medicine cups

(Left) Ceramic media of mixed sizes; (right) small stones of uniform hardness

Plastic strainer, liquid hand soap, bucket, scrub brush, mineral oil, spray bottle

Before taking a deep dive into the instructions for using your tumbler, you need to know about the materials you'll be using. The tumble-polishing process consists of using abrasives and polishes to first smooth the stones and then bring them to a glossy shine/polish (unless you choose to go with a matte or semigloss finish for some stones or jewelry pieces). You also need tumbling media or filler stones/pellets to help "carry" the abrasives and buffer the collisions of gemstones during tumbling. These materials are available at local and online lapidary supply stores and are generally sold by the pound.

Following are the different materials you'll need, organized in the sequence they will be used. The abrasives that you can acquire from lapidary suppliers are highly uniform, but the polish can be somewhat specialized. We highly recommend that you find the type of polishing compound shown in the table, as it greatly improves your chances of obtaining a high-gloss shine.

- **Coarse abrasive/grit (60–90 mesh)** Silicon carbide granules that are large enough to cause substantial removal of rough edges on hard gemstone materials and round out the overall shape of the stone

- **Medium abrasive/grit (120–220 mesh)** Silicon carbide granules that will remove some rough edges but will primarily smooth out the surfaces of the gemstones and remove any scratches or grooves from slab-saw or trim-saw cutting

- **Fine abrasive/grit (600 mesh)** Silicon carbide granules in a fine powder that is used for removing microscratches and preparing the gemstones for polishing

- **Aluminum oxide–based polishing compound** Aluminum oxide paste that polishes the gemstones through both micro-abrasion and melting, resulting in either a soft glow or high polish

- **Tumbling media** Marble- to pea-size ceramic pellets or small stones that are layered in with the gemstones you will be tumbling. If you use other stones, make sure they are the same hardness as the stones you are tumbling. These can be cleaned and reused many times. We recommend using a 1:1 mix of small and large ceramic pellets, as shown on the previous page. Don't use plastic pellets, as they will float to the top of your tumbler barrel and be ineffective.

The accessories below are necessary to make you more efficient. Set up some space in your lapidary storage and work area to keep them organized and handy for use during the tumbling process.

- **Liquid hand soap** to add with each tumbling stage and for your superclean tumbling stage

- **Large plastic colander** to place your stones into when emptying the tumbling barrel

- **Medium-size plastic containers,** one for each grit size/type and one for polishing compound

- **Small plastic measuring/medicine cups** for measuring grit and polishing compound, one for each grit size/type and one for polishing compound

- **Spray bottle** for adjusting moisture in vibratory tumblers

SETUP AND OPERATION

ROTARY TUMBLERS

The rotary tumbling process is low-maintenance, and you can attain a good skill level quickly. Before getting started, you need to decide on where you will be placing the machine. Rotary tumblers operate very quietly, so any enclosed room out of high-traffic areas is a good choice. In the summer, you can set yours up in a garage or outdoor shed, as long as there is available electric power. In colder climates, you'll need to bring your machine indoors when the temperature falls below freezing, or else the water will freeze and halt the tumbling process. A utility room or basement area with concrete flooring is your best bet. We also like to place an old towel (folded over) underneath the machine to absorb any possible leakage (though this is unusual) and to further dampen the sound. As a further precaution against leakage, set the machine in a shallow plastic tray.

VIBRATORY TUMBLERS

The vibratory tumbling process will at first seem to be higher-maintenance than rotary tumbling. This is primarily due to the short cycles between tumbling stages and the need to periodically check and adjust the moisture level inside the barrel. However, it truly is not much more work than rotary tumbling once you get the rhythm of the stages.

Because vibratory tumblers make more noise than rotary tumblers and make significant vibrations, we highly recommend that the machine be set up on a lower-level cement floor in an out-of-the-way place such as a utility room. To further dampen vibrations, place a folded towel or padded rug under the machine; this also keeps the machine from sliding across a smooth surface. Never cover the tumbler with any type of box to dampen sound, as the motor will overheat and potentially break down.

GETTING THE BEST TUMBLING RESULTS

Tumble-polishing is an astonishingly simple concept, and yet many, if not most, people get frustrated and don't even finish their first batch of rocks. The process consists of just a few tumbling stages (coarse-grinding, medium-grinding, fine-grinding, and polishing) and some simple additional steps (cleaning the stones, loading the barrel, running the tumbler). Despite its simplicity, tumble-polishing can be frustrating for beginners, especially when tumbled stones come out with loads of chips and fractures or with a dull luster, even though you followed the instructions you received when you purchased your tumbler. If you follow our simple approach and the corresponding tips and checklists we provide, you can avoid frustration and wasted time and materials.

Tumble-polishing is the subject of several complete books, so why do we think we can cover it in a chapter? First of all, experience. We've honed our skills over years of practice, and we've gleaned the essential information you need to help you master tumble-polishing and make your work more consistent and efficient. Second, this book is geared to amateur hobbyists, so we don't provide extraneous details on how polishing grits and compounds are formulated or specialty applications and materials that might come into play many years after you've learned to successfully tumble the most common rocks, gems, and cabochons. Finally, we've developed tables and checklists to accelerate your learning and help you produce beautifully polished gemstones and jewelry pieces. Best of all, on pages 42–43 we provide a comprehensive Tumbling Run Table, an easy-to-reference guide that you'll consult over and over again. It might be something you want to photocopy and then laminate to keep handy near your tumbling supplies.

TUMBLING STAGES

Finally, in this chapter we will describe three levels/styles of polishing: matte, semigloss, and fully polished. We describe all of these because some stones may be equally or even more beautiful when not taken to a high polish but rather left with a more natural finish. There are several significant advantages of a matte or semigloss finish, such as far shorter time to completion, lower cost, less polishing material used, and no fussing over that "ultimate high-gloss shine." As you become familiar with different types of gemstones and your own personal preferences, you can pick and choose whether matte, semigloss, or high polish will be best suited to a given project or lapidary product.

Tumbling progresses through multiple stages to arrive at a finished product. These stages gradually bring the gemstones from rough and sometimes jagged surfaces to increasingly smoother surface textures and finally to a high-gloss shine. The Tumbling Run Table below shows you how much grit or polish is required and the length of time the tumbler should be run for each stage. Note

TUMBLING RUN TABLE*

TUMBLER	STAGE 1: COARSE GRIT		STAGE 2: MEDIUM GRIT	
3-lb. Rotary	60–90 mesh		120–220 mesh	
	AMOUNT	TIME	AMOUNT	TIME
Standard	4 Tbsp.	10 days	4 Tbsp.	10 days
Simplified**	4 Tbsp.	20 days	Skip	
12- to 15-lb. Rotary	60–90 mesh		120–220 mesh	
	AMOUNT	TIME	AMOUNT	TIME
Standard	20 Tbsp. (1¼ cups)	10 days	20 Tbsp. (1¼ cups)	10 days
Simplified**	20 Tbsp. (1¼ cups)	20 days	Skip	
4-lb. Vibratory	60–90 mesh		120–220 mesh	
	AMOUNT	TIME	AMOUNT	TIME
Standard	Skip		1 Tbsp.	24 hours
			½ Tbsp. (1½ tsp.)	24 hours
Raytech TV-5	½ Tbsp. (1½ tsp.)	7 days	½ Tbsp. (1½ tsp.)	48 hours

* This chart is for stones with a Mohs hardness rating of 6 or 7. If you are tumbling

** It is possible with rotary tumblers to consolidate the rough/coarse-grind and by simply running the rotary tumbler for the combined amount of time for the days of running time). The benefits of doing this are fewer cleanup operations

that this chart is for stones with a Mohs hardness rating of 6 or 7, which is the majority of stones that we recommend for beginners. If you are tumbling softer stones, consider reducing the times by about 30%. And, more important, make sure you aren't mixing softer stones that are more than one hardness level apart (i.e., 6 and 7 are usually OK together, but you'll get better results if you do them separately, especially for the softer stones); the softer stones will wear down more, can get broken, and may not attain a high polish.

The table is simple to use: Select the tumbler type and tumbling stage you are on, and it tells you exactly how long to tumble your gemstones, plus the type and quantity of abrasive or polishing compound to use. If you want a matte finish, you can skip stages 3 and 4. If you want a semigloss finish, you can skip stage 4.

We provide details only for the tumblers featured in this book, but if you have a tumbler with a different capacity, it's not difficult to calculate how much abrasive and polish you'll need. As a rule, you can just scale up the amounts listed on the table. So if the table shows a 4-pound vibratory tumbler but you have a 10-pound vibratory tumbler, then simply multiply by 2.5 to get the correct amount of grit and polish for each cycle. (The run time will remain the same.) To keep things simple, after multiplying, you can round up to the next whole number.

STAGE 3: FINE GRIT		STAGE 4: POLISH	
600 mesh		Micro Alumina	
AMOUNT	TIME	AMOUNT	TIME
6 Tbsp.	10 days	6 Tbsp.	7 days
6 Tbsp.	10 days	6 Tbsp.	7 days
600 mesh		Micro Alumina	
AMOUNT	TIME	AMOUNT	TIME
24 Tbsp. (1½ cups)	10 days	24 Tbsp. (1½ cups)	7 days
24 Tbsp. (1½ cups)	10 days	24 Tbsp. (1½ cups)	7 days
600 mesh		Micro Alumina	
AMOUNT	TIME	AMOUNT	TIME
1 Tbsp.	24 hours	1 Tbsp.	24 hours
½ Tbsp. (1½ tsp.)	24 hours	½ Tbsp. (1½ tsp.)	24 hours
½ Tbsp. (1½ tsp.)	48 hours	½ Tbsp. (1½ tsp.)	48 hours

softer stones, consider reducing the times by about 30%.

medium-grind stages. You will achieve nearly the same quality of polished stones two stages (i.e., 10 days for stage 1, plus 10 days for stage 2, for a total of 20 and no need for medium grit.

43

Rough stones before tumbling

RESULTS PRODUCED BY EACH STAGE

1. **Rough/Coarse Grind** Removes sharp and angular surfaces, resulting in smooth and rounded stones

2. **Medium Grind** Provides a general smoothing or sanding of the stones and a bit more rounding

3. **Fine Grind** Creates a semigloss finish, with no additional rounding/shaping

4. **Superclean (optional)** You can run a "superclean" process in between any of the stages to remove remaining abrasive grit that may be hiding in small cracks or pits in the stones. This is especially helpful for stones with a lot of pitting (like agates). Just reload the tumbler barrel with the cleaned stones, tumbling media, water, and a small amount of liquid soap (a couple of squirts), and run the tumbler for at least an hour. Then empty and clean the stones before moving on to the next stage.

5. **Polish** Gives a high-gloss shine

Stones that are too jagged to tumble. If the stones have very sharp breaks and fractures, especially with harder stones like agates, you will never achieve a nice smooth surface.

After coarse grit for 20 days (rotary)

After fine grit

Polished

Polished with residue that needs a super-clean process

45

TUMBLING PROCESS STEP-BY-STEP

Below are the steps you'll repeat for each tumbling stage. Before you begin, set up the tumbler base in an out-of-the-way location on an old towel, and do a preliminary cleaning of your stones. We illustrate the process with the Raytech TV-5, a vibratory tumbler, but we also show a rotary tumbler barrel in steps 7–9 for reference (with rotary tumblers, you leave water in the barrel).

1. Select stones by size and hardness, with a mix of sizes.

2. Add water to the tumbler barrel.

3. Add a layer of small and medium stones, then put your larger stones on top of that layer.

4. Add a layer of small stones and tumbling media.

5. Add a layer of medium stones.

6. (vibratory) Add a layer of small stones and tumbling media to 75% full.

6. (rotary) Fill the tumbler with stones and water to 75% full using same layering sequence as vibratory.

7. (vibratory) Drain all water until stones are just damp.

7. (rotary) Drain excess water to just beneath the top layer of stones.

8. (vibratory) Place the tumbler barrel on the base. (For rotary, this is done after the water is drained, grit or polish has been added, and the barrel has been securely closed.)

9. (vibratory) Add coarse grit, spreading evenly across the top of the stones.

9. (rotary) Add grit evenly across the top of the stones, then securely attach and close the lid before putting on the base of the machine.

10. Place lid securely on barrel and tighten. **Run tumbler for prescribed number of days per Tumbling Run Table (pages 42–43).**

11a. Check moisture level every 4–8 hours to see if the stones are too dry (**vibratory only**).

11b. If stones are too dry, squirt in a little water to dampen stones, usually about three good squirts, or add about ½ Tbsp. with a medicine cup (**vibratory only**).

12. (Optional superclean) At end of each tumbling stage, add liquid hand soap, replace lid, and run for at least an hour.

13. Stones are cleaned up and ready for rinse.

14. Take outside for rinse and cleaning; this can also be done inside, but *avoid pouring water containing grit down the drain* (see page 50).

15. Gently empty barrel into colander.

16. Rinse barrel and stones.

17. Scrub barrel.

18. Scrub stones. **Remove and replace any chipped or broken stones to 75% full and move to next tumbling stage.**

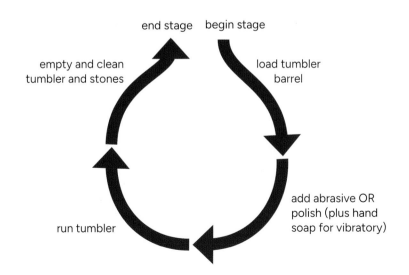

end stage   begin stage

empty and clean
tumbler and stones

load tumbler
barrel

run tumbler

add abrasive OR
polish (plus hand
soap for vibratory)

Each stage progresses through the same steps, starting with loading the barrel.

CLEAN THE STONES

Every experienced lapidary hobbyist will tell you that *cleaning is the most important step in the process* if you want to achieve the best-quality polished gemstones. Countless wasted hours and tumbling materials can be saved by taking a little extra time to thoroughly clean your gemstones and tumbling barrel before beginning each tumbling stage. This means removing all of the tumbling grit and any broken, chipped, and deeply pitted or fractured stones so that they don't scratch the surfaces of your gemstones as they get progressively smoother. The exception to this rule is that for the rough/coarse-grind stage, you will often start with stones that have rough and broken surfaces. To clean the stones properly, follow the steps below:

1. Fill a large plastic pail about half full with water and *gently* place your gemstones and tumbling media into the bucket. If you are moving between tumbling stages, you will be emptying the stones from your plastic colander into the bucket. Keep the stones immersed in water to reduce drying out and potential additional fracturing. Massage the stones with your hands and scrub any stones with small pits to remove sand, dirt, and abrasive particles.

2. As you get the stones cleaned/scrubbed, you can start placing them back into the tumbler barrel for the next stage (see "Load the Tumbler Barrel," below).

3. If you are moving between tumbling stages, remove any cracked, broken, or deeply pitted stones, and either discard them or put them back into your rough-rock bin. It is expected in the rough/coarse-grind stage that you will have stones with rough surfaces and broken edges.

4. Empty the bucket outside, *not down a sink or drain! Even small amounts of leftover tumbling abrasives or dirt and sand will eventually clog and close off your plumbing, resulting in major/expensive repairs.*

LOAD THE TUMBLER BARREL

The first important aspect of loading your tumbler barrel is that all of your stones and tumbling media must be of uniform hardness to ensure that the harder stones don't ruin the softer stones. The next critical aspect of the loading process is based on the concept of **balancing.** This simply means that you need to use a mixture of sizes in the gemstones, jewelry pieces, and tumbling media within the tumbling barrel. This is accomplished by placing the stones in several layers, starting with small stones and tumbling media, then larger stones (or jewelry pieces), and then medium stones; then repeat the sequence until the barrel is about 75% full, ending with a layer of small stones and tumbling media. *The 75% fill level is critical to ensure the proper movement of the stones during tumbling for both rotary and vibratory tumblers.*

Before you start placing the stones into the barrel, we suggest filling it one-third to half full with water. This is because, although the gemstones you'll be working with are very hard, they are still subject to cracking and chipping. By putting water into the barrel first and adding the stones gently, the stones will experience fewer collisions that can result in ugly fractures or blemishes.

The illustration below shows the layering sequence for a 3-to 4-lb. tumbler when your tumbler barrel is standing vertically. For larger (12- to 15-lb.) barrels, you'll be able to fit more layers, but remember to keep the large stones near the bottom and always end with a top layer of small stones and ceramic media. Some publications say you cannot tumble-polish stones larger than a golf ball, but this is untrue. In the 12- to 15-lb. barrel, you can fit stones up to tennis ball size—but you will be able to get only one or two stones of that size mixed into a well-layered mix of sizes. There should be a greater percentage of smaller stones and media than larger stones. A good overall mixture would be 20% larger stones, 40% medium stones, and 40% small stones and media. As to your choice of media, ceramic pellets are by far the best multipurpose option because they don't chip or fracture and can be used with a variety of stones with different hardness ratings. Ceramic pellets can be used over and over and will last at least 20 full tumbling runs.

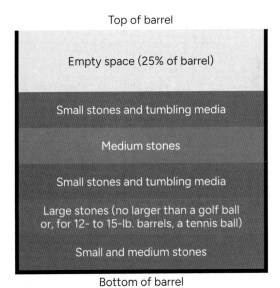

Top of barrel

Empty space (25% of barrel)

Small stones and tumbling media

Medium stones

Small stones and tumbling media

Large stones (no larger than a golf ball or, for 12- to 15-lb. barrels, a tennis ball)

Small and medium stones

Bottom of barrel

The layering sequence for two sets of layers when your tumbler barrel is standing vertically

Once you have completed loading the barrel to 75% full, check and adjust the water level (add more or pour out excess). For rotary tumblers, the water level should be just below the top layer of stones; you should be able to see the water level, but it should not cover the stones. Some settling will occur during the tumbling process, so it's important not to overfill with water or all the grit/polish will wash off the stones and settle at the bottom of the barrel.

ADD THE ABRASIVE/GRIT OR POLISHING COMPOUND

The Tumbling Run Table shows you how much abrasive/grit or polishing compound is needed for each tumbling stage and for each type and size of tumbler. Always add the abrasive/grit or polishing compound after you have adjusted the water/moisture level in the tumbling barrel. This is the very last thing you will do before closing the lid tightly and starting your tumbling run.

RUN THE TUMBLER FOR THE PRESCRIBED TIME PERIOD

The Tumbling Run Table (pages 42–43) will show you the recommended run times for each type of tumbler and each tumbling stage. Some books on tumbling advise that you need to periodically open your tumbler either to inspect the stones or to release trapped gases that may build up inside. Our recommendation for rotary tumblers is to *just let the tumbler run*. In fact, if you are stopping the tumbling process and opening the tumbler, the grit or polish will settle unevenly and/or harden in a layer at the bottom of the barrel. You can periodically check to ensure the tumbler isn't leaking and that you can hear the stones gently rolling in the tumbler—that's it!

EMPTY AND CLEAN THE TUMBLER BARREL

Open the tumbler and *gently* empty the contents of the tumbler barrel into a plastic colander set over a 5-gallon bucket (or set on the ground outside). Fill a second 5-gallon bucket half full with water. Gently empty the rocks from the colander into the bucket, and then perform the detailed cleaning process described on page 50. Clean the tumbler barrel with a small scrub brush or paper towels to remove any abrasive/grit from corners and seams. You want the barrel to be squeaky clean before moving to the next tumbling stage.

HELPFUL TIP Gentle handling of your gemstones and keeping them wet between stages is a huge factor in ensuring high-quality and high-polish results. Even though gemstones are very hard, many beautiful stones have been ruined by rough handling between tumbling stages.

HELPFUL TIP Abrasive/grit will settle at the bottom of the first 5-gallon bucket that you empty your tumbler into. Some people will periodically pour out the water (outside, of course) and then try to scrape out, dry, and reuse the residual grit. This is neither cost-effective nor reliable because you end up with a combination of partially worn-out grits of mixed coarseness (medium to fine). It's better to just discard this material.

OPTIONAL FINAL STEPS

These are performed only after the last tumbling stage. While these last steps are optional, they will make a huge difference by masking surface-level and even some sub-surface-level fractures and imperfections. This is especially helpful for stones like agates that often have lots of fracturing. Note that it's not as important for stones smaller than marble size because they tend to have far fewer fractures.

Use an Ultrasonic Cleaner

One way to remove embedded polish and grit is to use a stiff brush and warm soapy water. Another method is to use an ultrasonic cleaner such as the GemOro Sparkle Spa. Below is a short process for using this specific machine.

1. Put in 2 cups water.

2. Add 2 tablespoons EuroSonic solution.

3. Run the machine twice for 10 minutes each time.

4. Rinse the stones with a kitchen sink sprayer.

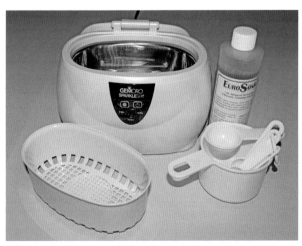

Ultrasonic cleaner and cleaning solution

Polished agates with embedded polish

Polished agates after cleaning in ultrasonic machine

Oil the Stones

After the stones are all cleaned and dried, place them in a small plastic bowl and soak them in mineral oil for three to five days. This step is especially important for stones such as agates that often have lots of fracturing. After the soak, use a fine strainer to drain the mineral oil off of the stones; note that the mineral oil can be used over and over again. After the oil is drained off, use a soft cloth rag to remove excess oil, and then use a second clean rag to do the process again. Finally, use paper towels to buff the stones to a high-gloss shine.

Agates with fractures before (above left) and after mineral oil application

Dry and Buff the Stones

Using a fine strainer, drain the mineral oil off the stones (note that the oil can be used over and over again). After the oil has drained off, use a soft rag to remove excess oil, then repeat with a second clean rag. Finally, use paper towels to buff the stones to a high gloss.

SPECIAL CONSIDERATIONS FOR VIBRATORY TUMBLERS

Vibratory tumbler processes differ from those used for rotary tumblers as outlined below:

First, load the tumbler barrel in the same manner as the rotary tumbler. Before adding your abrasive/grit or polish, drain all the water from the tumbler, leaving the stones dripping wet. Too much water will not allow the tumbling abrasives to bond effectively with the stones and perform the necessary grinding and smoothing. You can optionally add one or two pumps of liquid hand soap to improve the adhesion of the abrasive/grit or polish to the stones during tumbling.

During each tumbling stage, you must adjust the moisture level. Since vibratory tumblers don't have standing water, you need to periodically check that the slurry (water and tumbling abrasive or polishing compound) is maintaining a semiliquid consistency. If the slurry begins to appear dry or pasty, add approximately ½ tablespoon of water with either a medicine cup or a spray bottle. This should be done every 6–8 hours. Because vibratory tumblers sit vertically and are top loading, you can do the moisture check and adjustment process without stopping the machine (with the exception of the Raytech TV-5, which is discussed in more detail on the next page).

For vibratory tumblers, you should run each stage for 48 hours. At the end of the first 24 hours, you should adjust the moisture level, and then add more grit or polish as specified in the Tumbling Run Table (note that no extra grit or polish is needed for the TV-5). Then just continue to monitor and adjust the moisture level for another 24 hours.

Rapid Rinsing

At the completion of each tumbling stage, you'll find your cleanup goes a lot faster by doing a "rapid rinse" inside the tumbler. While the tumbler is still running, add one or two squirts of liquid soap and ½ cup of water, put the lid back on, and let the tumbler run for an hour. Then open and add enough water to cover the stones, and let the tumbler run for 10 more minutes. Turn off the tumbler and drain into a colander set over a 5-gallon bucket or on the ground outside.

Note: If you also have a rotary tumbler, you can perform coarse- and medium-grinding in a rotary tumbler and then perform the fine-grinding and polishing in the vibratory tumbler. With this approach, you can run your rough stones in a rotary tumbler for 15–20 days with coarse grit and then transition to the vibratory tumbler (skipping the medium-grit step).

HIGH-POLISH VS. MATTE OR SEMI-GLOSS FINISH

Agates that have been tumbled to a matte finish

Over time, more people have come to enjoy the soft luster of gemstones that have been tumbled to a matte or semigloss finish just as much as (or more than) highly polished stones. This is true both for stones that will simply be tumbled for display and for stones that will be used to make jewelry pieces. An additional application for a matte or semigloss finish is cutting whole agate nodules or stones that have a broken face and tumbling them for display.

Advantages of a Matte or Semigloss Finish vs. High Polish

- The amount of time you spend getting to a finish is shorter.

- You use less abrasive grit and no polishing compound, so the cost is lower.

- There is less fussing over the tumbling process details (especially the meticulous cleaning) since you aren't going for a high-gloss shine.

- Your "housekeeping" efforts between tumbling stages are reduced. In fact, for rotary tumblers we suggest a two-step process consisting of an extended coarse/rough grind and a fine grind.

SPECIAL INSTRUCTIONS FOR THE RAYTECH TV-5

The Raytech TV-5 tumbler is the only vibratory tumbler that can perform coarse-grinding of rough stones, which makes it a full-service tumbler; it's also an affordable machine for beginners. We've added this special section for the TV-5 because its setup and operation differ from that of other vibratory tumblers. Keep in mind that the TV-5, like other vibratory tumblers, is much noisier than rotary tumblers and needs to be on a ground-level floor that can absorb the vibrations.

We strongly recommend that you purchase the TV-5 kit, which includes a second tumbling barrel for coarse- and medium-grit processing to avoid carry-over into the subsequent fine-grit and polishing stages. The kit also includes specially formulated tumbling grits and polishing compounds. The manufacturer's instructions reference these grits and compounds, but we recommend using standard grits and polishes, as outlined below. These standard materials will yield comparable results and will be easier and cheaper to acquire from lapidary suppliers (both online and local).

SETUP OF THE RAYTECH TV-5

Before jumping into the detailed process instructions, let's cover machine setup.

- Steps 1 and 2 need to be done only once, when you first get the machine. You can purchase and put on a locking nut with a nylon insert to prevent the rod from coming loose; this would be in place of the regular metal nut that comes with the machine.

- Steps 3 and 4 need to be done at the beginning of each tumbling stage.

- Steps 5–8 are done multiple times during each tumbling stage to adjust moisture in the barrel. Note that you must purchase a wide rubber washer and regular metal nut that will be attached when placing the lid on the barrel—*these are essential to ensure proper operation of the tumbler.*

1. Unbox the TV-5 machine base, threaded rod, and metal nut. Get ready to assemble the base of the tumbler.

2. Attach threaded rod to base. Screw the threaded rod into the base and use pliers or a vise-grip to tighten. Slide the metal washer over the threaded rod, and then screw on and tighten the metal nut with pliers or a wrench.

3. Gather the parts needed to attach tumbler barrel to base. You'll use all these parts each time you load or unload the tumbling barrel and whenever you need to adjust the moisture level while the machine is running, so keep them handy wherever the machine will be used. Note that you need to purchase the wide rubber washer and an additional metal nut.

4. Attach barrel to base. Slide the loaded tumbler barrel over the rod, then attach one of the rubber-coated nuts and tighten first with your fingers and then with pliers.

5. Place lid tightly on barrel, with parts ready to attach the lid securely. This is the secret sauce of running the TV-5 successfully. A secure lid equals continuous action and no spinning loose from the base of the machine.

6. Put the large rubber washer on the rod, and then tighten the second rubber nut. Place the lid onto the tumbler barrel and make sure there's a tight seal all the way around. Put a larger-diameter rubber washer over the rod so that the pressure of the rubber-coated nut is more distributed on the plastic lid; this helps create a tighter seal and reduces the chance of the lid getting cracked. Attach the second rubber-coated nut above the lid and tighten with both your fingers and then with a pair of pliers.

7. Put on metal nut and tighten. Attach metal nut above rubber nut and tighten with a wrench.

8. Fully assembled

FULL TUMBLING PROCESS SPECIFIC TO THE RAYTECH TV-5

Most of these steps are consistent with the regular vibratory tumbler processes; however, there are some things that are specific to the TV-5, so we thought it would be more convenient for you to have all the instructions in one place.

Coarse-Grit Stage

1. Load the barrel with water and stones to approximately 75% full.

2. Drain all water, leaving the stones just damp; if water pools at the bottom of the barrel, the stones won't move properly, causing them to dry out completely on the top portion of the barrel.

3. Sprinkle on ½ tablespoon of 60- to 90-mesh silicon carbide abrasive (also referred to as coarse grit).

4. Slide the barrel over the rod that's attached to the machine, and attach the bowl to the tumbler base using one of two rubber-coated nuts; first tighten as much as possible with your fingers, and then use pliers to further tighten.

5. Secure the lid on the tumbler; it must have a tight seal all the way around. Put on the second rubber washer; tighten it as much as possible with your fingers, and then use pliers to further tighten. Finally, put on a regular metal nut and tighten it using a wrench. This might seem rather intensive, but these steps are critical to keep the barrel or lid from coming loose, resulting in rotational motion, which results in no actual tumbling and drying out of the stones. When the machine is running optimally, the stones should be vibrating and rolling/folding in toward the center while slowly rotating around the barrel.

6. Every 4–8 hours, turn the machine off, open the lid, and check the moisture level. If the slurry is thick and pasty, add ½ tablespoon of water, or use a spray bottle and squirt a fine mist two to three times onto the top layer of stones. If

there is too much water in the barrel, remove the barrel and drain excess into a bucket before restarting the tumbler. Secure the lid back onto the barrel.

7. Turn the machine on and check the tumbling action to ensure the rocks are being tumbled thoroughly and consistently. Run the tumbler in this manner for three to four days.

8. Add two to three pumps of liquid hand soap and run for an hour, then add 2 cups of water and run for another hour.

9. Empty the bowl and clean the stones and barrel thoroughly. Remove any chipped or broken stones.

10. Run a superclean cycle, as described on page 44, and then repeat step 9.

Medium-Grit Stage

1. Reload the tumbler barrel with the stones and water (add additional tumbling media as needed so that the barrel is 75% full).

2. Drain the water and sprinkle on ½ tablespoon of 120- to 220-mesh silicon carbide grit (sometimes referred to as medium grit).

3. Attach the barrel and lid as described in steps 3–5 of the coarse-grit stage.

4. Repeat steps 6 and 7 of the coarse-grit stage for two full days, and then perform steps 8–10 of the coarse-grit stage.

At this point, you will switch to the secondary barrel for finishing and polishing. Some people prefer to switch after the fine-grit stage and use the secondary barrel only for polishing.

Fine-Grit Stage

1. Reload the barrel with the stones and water (add additional tumbling media as needed so that the barrel is 75% full).

2. Drain the water and sprinkle on ½ tablespoon of 600-mesh silicon carbide grit (sometimes referred to as fine grit).

3. Attach the barrel and lid as described in steps 4 and 5 of the coarse-grit stage.

4. Repeat steps 6 and 7 of the coarse-grit stage for two full days, and then perform steps 8–10 of the coarse-grit stage.

Polish Stage

1. Reload the tumbler barrel with the stones and water (add additional tumbling media as needed so that the barrel is 75% full).

2. Drain the water and sprinkle on ½ tablespoon of 120- to 220-mesh silicon carbide grit (sometimes referred to as medium grit).

3. Attach the barrel and lid as described in steps 3–5 of the coarse-grit stage.

4. Repeat steps 6 and 7 of the coarse-grit stage for two full days, and then perform steps 8–10 of the coarse-grit stage.

TV-5 TROUBLESHOOTING

If the rocks aren't moving correctly in the barrel or are drying out, these are some things that might need to be adjusted:

Problem: Stones are rotating around the barrel and not folding inward.

- Tighten the rubber-coated nut that attaches the barrel to the base of the machine with your fingers and then pliers.

- Make sure the lid has a tight seal all the way around the rim and is attached securely with both the rubber-coated nut and supplemental metal nut.

- Be sure that the machine is sitting on something soft, such as a rubber-backed carpet floor mat or a folded towel.

Problem: Stones are dry on the top layer.

- Check to see if there's any water pooling in the bottom of the barrel. If there is, pour it out, then run the machine for a few minutes and stop to check if the top layers are getting moist.

- If there's no water pooling, then use a spray bottle and mist three times to moisten the stones, then run the machine for a few minutes and stop to check if the top layers are getting moist.

- Too much or too little tumbling material (stones)

- Optimal results come when the barrel is 75% full. If you don't have enough stones, you can substitute additional media or other stones that are similar in hardness to what you are tumbling.

Problem: Stones in barrel are riding up to a higher level on one side of barrel.

- Make sure the base of the machine is level. You can use a shim or a small towel/rag to slightly elevate the base of the machine on the side where the stones are riding up higher.

TUMBLING TIPS SUMMARY

Here, we highlight some of the most critical tips from this chapter that will make your hobby enjoyable and successful.

- A good-quality tumbler is well worth the investment. Inexpensive tumblers wear out quickly, produce poor results, and make excessive noise.

- For each tumbling grit or polish, use a separate plastic measuring cup (these are cheap; buy a stack of 2-oz. plastic medicine cups for a couple of dollars and you'll be set for life).

- Use ceramic tumbling media or a variety of low-quality stones of the same type and hardness you are tumbling. Do not use plastic pellets, as they will float and be ineffective.

- Place your tumbler, especially vibratory tumblers like the Raytech TV-5, in a low-traffic area where the noise will not disturb others. Place an old towel or piece of old carpet or two underneath the tumbler base to catch any leakage and dampen the sound.

- Keep your grits and polishes in a cool, dry place in tightly closed containers (inexpensive plastic containers with locking lids or ziplock bags are fine).

- *Never empty the tumbler barrel down the drain.* The grit will turn into a cementlike mixture, settle in your drain traps, harden, and prevent water flow. This can result in a multithousand-dollar plumbing repair!

- In warm weather, "dirty rinse" outside with a hose and colander; in cold weather, you can do this inside with a colander and a large plastic bucket.

- *Clean your stones thoroughly between tumbling stages.* Put them in a bucket of water and scrub them with a small brush (keep them wet). Pay extra attention to stones with deep pits where abrasives can get trapped (or you might choose to discard these). Do a "cleansing run"—just soap and water for an hour or two—before the polishing stage.

- Clean the barrel and lid thoroughly between stages. A spray bottle is great for getting grit out of the inner rim of the barrel. Using paper towels to rub out the inside after the barrel has been rinsed is also a good idea.

- Handle rocks with care to avoid cracking and chipping. Partially fill your tumbler barrel with water (one-third to one-fourth full) first, then carefully place stones into the barrel. When 75% full, check the water level and add or pour off water as needed. When removing stones, pour the stones out slowly and only use a gentle shaking motion to remove if you cannot get your hand into the tumbler barrel. A plastic spoon or spatula can also be used to scoop out the stones.

- Don't mix stones of more than one level of difference in hardness in the same barrel; ideally, they should be equally hard. For example, stones that are 6 and 7 on the Mohs scale are usually OK together, but you'll get better results if you do them separately, especially with the softer (6) stones; the softer stones will wear down more, can get broken, and may not attain a high polish.

- Mix the sizes of stones within a single batch to maximize tumbling and grinding/sanding/polishing action.

- If you are tumbling jewelry pendant slabs/cabs, layer small stones or tumbling media in between each layer of slabs/cabs. Usually a ratio of 75% tumbling media and filler stones to 25% slabs/cabs will give good results.

- Between tumbling stages, remove any stones that are broken or have rough/sharp edges.

- Don't overtend your tumbler—especially rotary tumblers. Turning the tumbler off and on can cause the grit to settle in a clump at the bottom. Some old books on tumbling say you will get gas buildup and possibly even explosions if you don't periodically open the lid of your tumbler, but *this is exceedingly rare, making periodic checks unnecessary.*

- *Keep a checklist or log of your tumbling activities* and your own personal tips and tricks. This is especially valuable when you are getting started.

- *Garbage in, shiny garbage out.* Don't expect to turn low-grade stones into beautiful stones simply by tumble-polishing them.

- For rotary tumblers, you can do a one-step process for a matte finish and a three-step process for polishing by running the coarse grit for 20–25 days and then skipping the medium-grit stage. This saves grit, cleaning time, and overall effort.

- For most hobbyists, detailed inspection of stones between tumbling stages is unnecessary. You can feel and see broken, cracked, and deeply pitted stones with your bare eyes and hands. And, if you follow the steps in this book carefully, there's no need to inspect the stones with a magnifier to see if they have reached the desired smoothness.

- *Make sure to keep the tumbler running to ensure the grit doesn't solidify in the barrel.* In general, it's an important practice to keep the tumbler running until just before emptying.

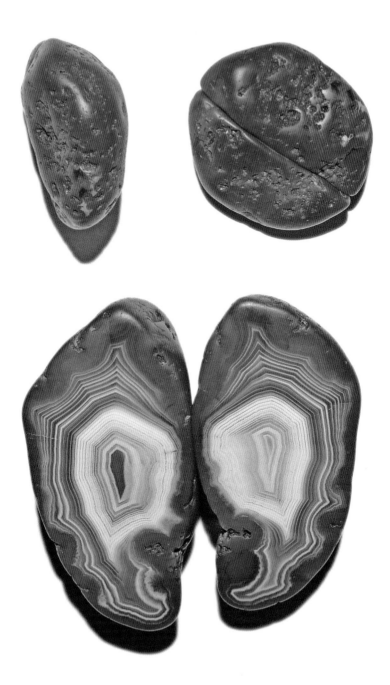

CHAPTER 4: CUTTING

OVERVIEW

The first step in making many lapidary products, including necklace pendants, is **slabbing**, or cutting your gemstones into slabs (slices). Slabbing is done with a lapidary saw, which is also used for cutting slabs into **cabochons** (shapes) and rough-cutting (removing rough or uneven sections from gemstones). **Rough-cutting** is often necessary before polishing a gemstone and is also useful if you have a whole gemstone you want to slice open (such as a whole agate nodule) and subsequently polish.

Cutting gemstones involves gemstone selection, starting the cut, rocking and rolling (which helps make a clean cut and avoid damage to the saw blade), and cleaning up any rough areas from the cut. Stones must then be cleaned before they can be further shaped. Gemstone selection and careful use of the saw are key to successful cutting. By following our tips, you're more likely to have success.

LAPIDARY EQUIPMENT AND SUPPLIES NEEDED

Slabbing and cutting require a lapidary saw. Lapidary saws can cut through very hard gemstone materials and use either an oil-based or a water-based lubricant (which also acts as a coolant and helps to flush away debris). We recommend using high-quality diamond-coated, sintered-rim saw blades to obtain clean cuts and make the best use of your precious gemstones. Note that some saws come with blades that are of poor quality; they might be silicon carbide blades or lower-quality diamond-coated blades that degrade the cutting ability of the saw. This is why we recommend that you purchase an additional blade when you get a new saw. You might still be able to use the manufacturer-supplied blades for things like trimming precut slabs.

TIME REQUIREMENTS

It doesn't take long to make a cut through a stone, just 30–60 seconds for smaller stones and up to 3 minutes for larger gemstones with a higher hardness rating (such as agates). If you will be cutting several slabs out of a single stone, simply multiply the time needed to make one cut by the number of cuts you need to make.

RECOMMENDED EQUIPMENT AND SUPPLIES

There are technically two kinds of saws for cutting slabs: **slab- and rock-cutting saws** and **trim saws**. Trim saws have less power than slab- and rock-cutting saws, which have continuous-duty motors. You can use either to **trim-cut** precut slabs or to cut small (up to 1 inch thick) to medium (1–2 inches thick) rocks, depending on the hardness of the stones (small stones with hardness 6 or 7, and medium stones with a hardness of 5 or less). For amateur hobbyists, you might need only a trim saw if you intend to use it almost exclusively for trim-cutting precut slabs, such as those used for making jewelry pieces; you don't need anything more than a 6-inch blade when working with slabs that are no more than ½-inch thick.

While many saws can work with either water or oil, oil reduces friction so you can get cleaner cuts and have less chance of chipping or fracturing your materials. **Rockhound oil** is nontoxic but can be messy, and you'll need to purchase more from time to time. The oil is relatively inexpensive, so cleanup is probably the bigger issue, but if you take the proper precautions (see page 13), you can prevent much of the mess. You might choose to use water for trim-cutting slabs where you don't need as much cutting efficiency and oil when you are cutting slabs from rock chunks like tiger's-eye or jaspers, or when cutting whole rocks like agates. If you use water for cutting, *always make sure to drain the reservoir after each use to the point where the blade isn't immersed* or it will rust and corrode your expensive diamond blades! Products like Gem Lube and Lubri Kool can be added to water to inhibit rust and corrosion.

With all of these points taken into consideration, we recommend the following lapidary saws:

The Hi-Tech Diamond 6-inch trim saw is our primary recommendation strictly as a trim saw. It uses water as a lubricant but can also be used with oil. It has a ¼-horsepower variable-speed motor that provides substantially less cutting power than our other two recommended 6-inch saws. If you intend to do a lot of rough rock cutting, this saw will not be up to the task, but it's a super lightweight, portable saw that is perfect for trim-cutting slabs. It's also quieter than the other two saws we recommend.

HELPFUL TIP When using water as your lubricant, make sure to drain the reservoir after each use so your blades don't get corroded or rusty.

The Johnson Brothers Rock Rascal is our primary recommendation as a 6-inch combination rock-cutting and trim saw. It can be used with water or oil, though we recommend water because it's much easier to clean up. Covington Engineering and Kingsley North 6-inch rock-cutting and trim saws work primarily

Hi-Tech Diamond 6-inch trim saw
RICHARD PAUPORE

Johnson Brothers Rock Rascal
6-inch slab and rock-cutting saw
RICHARD PAUPORE

with rockhound oil. All of these saws have continuous-duty AC motors that deliver plenty of power for cutting slabs out of whole rocks and for trim cutting. So, while these saws are labeled as trim saws, they can reliably cut 1- to 3-inch-thick rocks. You'll pay a premium for the Kingsley and Covington saws, but that's because they come with a more powerful motor and more sturdy construction, and they are better designed for using oil as a cutting lubricant.

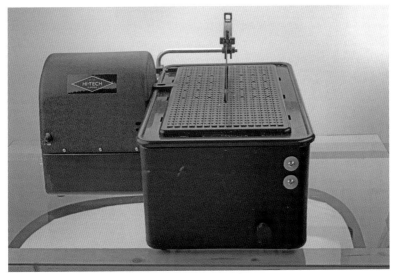

Hi-Tech Diamond 10-inch slab and rock-cutting saw   RICHARD PAUPORE

The Hi-Tech Diamond 10-inch slab and rock-cutting saw can use either water or rockhound oil. It has a ⅓-horsepower continuous-duty AC motor (fixed speed) that delivers plenty of power for cutting slabs out of whole rocks and for trim cutting. It reliably cuts 1- to 4-inch-thick rocks.

A NOTE ON EQUIPMENT

Some people try to use equipment that's made for carpentry and home improvement projects to perform lapidary tasks. Perhaps the most common such example is using a tile saw to cut rocks. Even when using a good lapidary blade, there are many problems with this, the most important of which is safety. Because you don't have a solid cutting surface or cutting table, you have less control over the stone. Many people have had serious injuries and broken windows due to rocks flying out. Also, because you have less control, you are more likely to damage or destroy your gemstone materials.

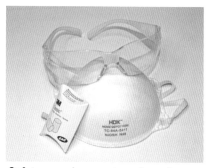
Safety goggles, mask, and earplugs

SETUP AND OPERATION

SAFETY

You might be wondering about the safety of lapidary trim saws. Surprisingly, the diamond saw blades have continuous rims, and it's the crushed diamonds that do the cutting, not a sharp steel or carbide blade, so they rarely break the surface of your skin; thus, you won't need to wear protective gloves. However, we do recommend wearing wraparound protective eyewear and earmuffs (or earplugs). As long as you take these precautions, cutting gemstone slabs is safe and relatively easy when you have the right equipment and supplies. Please also see the note about silicosis on page 8.

Saw blade with sintered rim

SAW BLADES

Your choice of blade is just as important as your choice of saw. Rock saws can cut through rock because their blades are coated with materials that are even harder than the gemstones they cut. There are two types of blade coatings: silicon carbide and pulverized diamonds. Silicon carbide is the same material as rock-tumbling grit. Saw blades with a silicon carbide coating were once popular, but thanks to improvements in materials technology, blades coated with pulverized diamonds are now much more popular.

Don't waste your money on silicon carbide blades. While they are cheaper, you get what you pay for. A diamond blade will last much longer and will cut much faster. It will also make cleaner cuts than a silicon carbide one; this helps protect your precious gemstones from additional chips, fractures, or deep grooves.

About Diamond Blades

In a process called sintering, crushed diamonds are applied to specialized metals. This results in a narrow strip or rim of diamond coating around the edge of the blade. When the blade is used, this edge gradually wears away. When the gold-colored sintered portion is gone, it's time to purchase a new blade. As noted above, sintered diamond saw blades have a continuous rim (no jagged cutting teeth), so they are vastly safer than blades used for carpentry and woodworking.

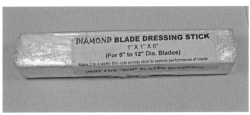

To get the maximum life out of your diamond blades, periodically make a couple of thin cuts through a saw blade dressing stick. To make things simple, do this every time you finish using the saw for the day.

Recommended Blade Thickness

Diamond blades differ in thickness. We recommend a .032-inch blade; this medium-thickness blade is suitable for cutting the gemstones in this book. Thinner blades have their advantages—they waste less gemstone material and can give a more precise cut—but they are more subject to warping and hence require more care to use.

LUBRICANTS

If your rock saw requires an oil-based lubricant, it will almost always be best to use a product known as lapidary or rockhound oil, which is available from all lapidary supply companies. The best brands are mineral based (rather than petroleum distillate based), are neutral in terms of odor, and feature excellent cooling properties that extend the life of your saw blade and your saw.

Rockhound oil
RICHARD PAUPORE

CUTTING

69

MAKING THE BEST CUT

First, you need to decide what you'll be creating. Are you simply cutting a whole agate nodule in half, or are you cutting away the rough surface of a stone and then face-polishing the cut surfaces? Or perhaps you are creating jewelry slabs or slices.

If you're creating jewelry, there are two different ways to use your saw. You can create either **whole-stone, natural-shape slabs,** or **rough slabs to be cut and shaped.** Agates are commonly cut into natural-form slabs; while you have the option of trimming whole-stone agate slabs into symmetrical shapes (ovals, for example), many people prefer to leave them in a natural shape or a form that follows the shape of the stone. Petrified wood and jasper are two materials that are commonly cut into rough slabs and then cut into symmetrical shapes; unlike agates, these tend to come in large chunks or blocks, so they don't lend themselves to small, natural-shape jewelry pendants.

Once you've decided on what you want to create, you need to figure out how to get the best rock slabs from your gemstones. This aspect of gemstone cutting is highly intuitive, meaning there is no perfect way to decide how and where to cut into your materials. You will develop your own techniques as you spend more time with your favorite gemstones.

Of course, the best way to learn is simple: practice. We recommend practicing on lower-quality materials and specimens before you start cutting higher-grade gemstones. This will get you comfortable with using the saw, and it's a great way to practice other important parts of the sawing process. The following guidelines will help determine how to cut, your cutting angle, and the width of your cuts.

DON'T WASTE MATERIAL

Before you cut, estimate how many slabs or slices can be obtained from the stone. If you're cutting multiple slices, consider how thick they need to be for your planned use. For jewelry pieces, the thickness should be ¼ to ⅜ inch, or 7–8 millimeters; you can go somewhat thinner, but this thickness allows you to create a raised and rounded surface once you start working the piece.

CUTTING A WHOLE STONE

Cutting whole stones is tricky, especially if there are no visible features, such as patterns, on the outside to guide you. If there is no visible pattern, cut the stone across its widest point. This will give you the largest possible slabs, if that's how you intend to cut it; it also will expose the maximum amount of surface area if you are polishing the face of each half. If there is exposed pattern (as often happens with agates), you should cut at an angle that highlights the pattern.

Cutting off end to square up

REMOVE FLAWED AREAS AND SQUARE UP THE SIDES

Always remove the rough and fractured sections of stone first, but remove the smallest amount possible; if you discover additional fracturing after the first cut, the stone is probably not suited for lapidary work. Depending on the thickness of the stone, you might need to cut away the rough exterior surfaces on both sides first to get multiple interior slabs with flat surfaces.

Exposed face of a beautiful Montana agate

HIGHLIGHT THE MOST ATTRACTIVE FEATURES

Cut at an angle that exposes the most striking features. You may need to make an **exploratory cut** near the outer surface on one side of the stone; this can help you determine what subsequent cuts will yield slabs that best highlight the stone's natural colors and patterns.

STARTING A CUT

When cutting away the rough exterior surface, start from the side of the stone where you will be cutting away the most material; this helps the saw blade get a solid entry and "bite" into the stone. This will also create a smoother, more even surface and will make sanding and polishing your gemstones easier later.

HOW TO HOLD A STONE WHILE CUTTING

Some saws have a pre-installed vise and guide bar that can be used to hold your gemstones in place while you push them through the rotating saw blade. While these types of setups can be useful for cutting large pieces of gemstone material or for high-precision, high-volume cutting, they are unnecessary for hobbyists, and we will not address them in this book. Additionally, using such vises and guides makes it more likely that you'll break off chunks of stone at the front or back of the cutting surface, as you can't use the rocking and rolling technique (see page 74) but instead have to cut straight through from front to back.

The best way to hold a gemstone is much simpler: use your hands. You will generally hold the stones between the thumb, forefinger, and middle finger of both hands in something of a pincer/claw arrangement. (*Note:* Always use protective equipment and follow the safety measures described on page 68, protective eyewear being the most critical.)

Start your cut on the wide end of the stone and hold the gemstone securely.

CUTTING PROCESS STEP-BY-STEP

STEP 1: START THE CUT

Once you have a good hold on the stone, guide it straight into the saw blade. Avoid exerting any side-to-side pressure, as this bends or tilts the blade and will eventually cause it to warp. This is also more likely to cause your gemstone material to fracture or break as the blade comes through the last portion of it.

Press the stone forward in a straight line.

STEP 2: STAY ON A CONTINUOUS LINE

Once you've started cutting, make sure to exert pressure along the same line that you started. Again, trying to alter the angle or cutting line could damage both your gemstone material and the saw blade. Exert only enough pressure to keep the stone moving forward or "through the blade." If the blade is slowing down or stopping, ease up and "let the saw guide you."

STEP 3: SHARPEN YOUR BLADE

If the blade begins to bog down and have difficulty cutting your stones, it might need to be sharpened. A saw dressing stick will remove buildup and expose a new layer of diamonds on the sintered rim. Just cut three to four thin (1- to 2-millimeter thick) slices. Also, remember that once the gold-colored diamond sintered portion of the blade is gone, the blade will no longer cut; this is true even if only a small portion of the rim is down to metal, but usually your blades will wear relatively evenly.

Sharpen your blade with a saw blade dressing stick.

Rock backward so bottom portion is being cut.

Rock forward so top portion is being cut.

STEP 4: ROCK AND ROLL

After your stone is at least halfway through the blade, you should begin to gently roll (rotate) the stone backward and forward as you guide it through the blade in three stages:

1. Roll the front (farthest from you) edge of the stone back toward you slightly, allowing the blade to cut through more of the underside. When you've cut through about 75% of the underside, roll the stone back to its original position.

2. Roll the back edge of the stone forward, cutting through more of the top side of the stone, until there is only a thin strip of uncut material left between the cuts on the top and bottom.

3. Roll the stone back to its original position, and then slowly cut through the remaining material as you very gently rock the stone back and forth. As you do so, try to apply only slight pressure against the saw blade, gradually moving the stone forward.

Learning this trick takes practice, but it's important because it makes it far less likely that your gemstones will break or fracture as the blade comes through the last portion of the stone.

STEP 5: CLEAN UP THE CUT

When you have cut completely through your stone, you might notice that there is a slight lip or burr on the edge of one or both pieces. You can gently place the stone against the saw blade near the lip, and rotate the stone slowly to cut away

Remove any burrs or ridges from the edges of the stone.

the excess. This material can also be ground off or tumbled away, but it's sometimes best to remove more significant protrusions with the saw.

ADDITIONAL CONSIDERATIONS

SLAB THICKNESS

It will take some time and practice to gauge how thick your cut will be when cutting slabs. If you're planning on drilling all the way through a slab (called face-drilling) to make a jewelry piece, remember that drilling through thick gemstones is costly (drill bits are expensive) and time-consuming; if you're planning on using a piece for jewelry and you won't be doing any grinding with a flat lap or cabber, we specifically recommend a maximum slab thickness of ¼ inch, or 6–7 millimeters.

CUTTING LARGE STONES

If your stone is substantially thicker than the height of the saw blade above the table (which is 2 inches for a 6-inch saw blade and 4 inches for a 10-inch saw blade), you will have to roll the stone 180 degrees to be able to fully cut through it. Stones that require this might be too large for the saw; cutting them can result in uneven wear on your diamond blade, and it could even bend the blade, rendering your expensive diamond blade useless!

CLEANING YOUR STONES

Before putting any stones in a tumbler or working with them on a flat lap or cabber, we recommend thoroughly cleaning your stones, especially if you've cut them using rockhound oil or other coolant additives. It's best to clean batches of cut stones all at once, as this makes your work more efficient. Soak the stones with a grease-fighting dish detergent in warm water. Gently massage them, rinse off the soap, and then towel dry.

CUTTING TIPS SUMMARY

- Safety with rock saws is relatively simple: Always wear a good pair of protective glasses, and to help control dust, always use a lubricant when cutting and work in a well-ventilated area. Noise-dampening earmuffs and a protective mask are the only other things you might need.

- Rocking and rolling your stones gently in three stages will result in fewer breaks and fractures and prolong the life of your saw blade.

- Never apply sideways pressure on the blade while sawing gemstone material; this will warp the blade and may fracture your gemstones.

- To keep the peace, find an out-of-the-way place to do your rock cutting and consider the hour of day that you enjoy your sawing.

- Don't try to cut stones that are too large for your saw blade, as this tends to cause uneven wear on the expensive diamond blades. As a rule, the stone should not be thicker than the height of the portion of the saw blade that's above the surface of the saw table (2 inches for a 6-inch saw blade and 4 inches for a 10-inch saw blade).

- The importance of using a high-quality sintered diamond blade cannot be overemphasized. While these blades range from $45 for a 6-inch blade to $65 for a 10-inch blade, when used properly they will have a very long life and produce hundreds (if not thousands) of cuts. Inexpensive rock saw blades and tile-saw blades take three to four times as long to produce cuts (especially for slabs) and result in much more scratching and scarring; these blemishes are difficult to remove with tumbling and grinding.

- To get the most life out of your diamond saw blades, we recommend purchasing an inexpensive saw blade dressing stick. Periodically make a couple of thin cuts through the dressing stick. To make things simple, do this every time you finish using the saw, as your last cut of the day!

- If you are using water without any coolant additives, make sure to *drain your saw reservoir immediately after use so the blade doesn't rust or corrode.*

CHAPTER 5:
CABOCHON MAKING
AND FACE-POLISHING

OVERVIEW

Cabochon making involves using several lapidary processes to convert rough gemstone materials into symmetrical shapes for jewelry pieces, such as necklaces, bracelets, and cuff links. Face-polishing is less complex but uses most of the same machines and supplies and has many of the same steps. Many people enjoy creating face-polished stones because they get a highly polished surface that highlights the most beautiful colors and pattern while leaving the rest of the stone in its rough, natural state. We provide process details for each, along with several ways to simplify things and make you more efficient.

Making cabochons combines most of the lapidary techniques described in this book, including cutting, grinding, dome-polishing, and (optionally) tumbling and drilling. The table on page 89 lists the major steps required to make cabochons and face-polish stones, and which of the steps are required. The process begins with grinding away excess material and creating a rounded, or domed, surface. This is followed by sanding away the scratches and grooves left from the grinding process and then further smoothing the surface. The polishing stage is then used to create a glossy surface.

Face-polished Teepee Canyon agate (in matrix)

As with other lapidary processes and products, everything starts with choosing lapidary-grade gemstone materials. This is especially critical with cabochon making given the time requirements and the fact that the finished pieces will be used for jewelry. Additionally, patience and careful inspection of your work are key. While it's possible to rush through the polishing process, this often produces poor-quality results. At first these processes might seem intimidating, so we recommend starting with simple shapes, like ovals, and smaller stones for face-polishing. Once you gain experience, you'll find yourself inventing and creating your own shapes and styles.

LAPIDARY EQUIPMENT AND SUPPLIES NEEDED

The primary machines required for cabochon making and face-polishing are flat laps (flat lapidary grinders-polishers) and cabbers. The first uses discs that lie horizontally (or flat), and the second uses wheels that are vertical. The discs and wheels are both coated with diamond abrasives of varying coarseness that shape, sand, smooth, and polish your gemstones. Saws are used to trim away excess material, and tumblers can be used to "finish" your stones.

TIME REQUIREMENTS

The simplest of cabochons (natural shape, flat on both sides) will take only a few minutes to get things ready for finishing in a tumbler. More complex pieces, such as those that need to be fitted to a premade metal bezel, can take up to 30 minutes. Working your pieces in groups reduces the amount of switching between discs if you're using a flat lap or slant lap machine. For face-polishing, you can complete a small (1- to 2-inch-diameter) stone in about 10–15 minutes, whereas larger stones with more surface flaws might take 15–30 minutes. Again, doing multiple stones at once will save time. You can further increase your efficiency by finishing your pieces in a tumbler; this is especially true for cabochons.

RECOMMENDED EQUIPMENT AND SUPPLIES

Both types of machines—flat laps and cabbers—follow nearly identical process steps and use diamond-coated discs or wheels to produce finished pieces with a high-gloss polish. The table on the opposite page compares the advantages of each. There's a third type of machine called a slant lap or slant cabber. It's identical to the flat lap, except that the discs are mounted at a 45-degree angle, which means you won't need to tilt your head and neck as much to view your stone or jewelry pieces against the grinding and polishing discs.

Because of the advantages listed above, for beginners we recommend using a flat lap or slant lap. These machines are incredibly easy to use and will stand the test of time. We recommend an 8-inch flat lap because the 6-inch limits the size of

FLAT LAPS AND CABBERS COMPARED

ADVANTAGES OF FLAT LAPS	
Lightweight and portable	Simple and quick to learn how to use
At $650 for a complete setup, an 8" flat lap is less than half the cost of a smaller 6" cabber.	
Up to 3 people can work on an 8" flat lap at the same time.	
Lower cost for discs, especially when using top plates with peel-off pressure-sensitive adhesive (PSA) paper and your original backer plates	
Extremely efficient when running batches of jewelry pieces or multiple stones for face-polishing	
ADVANTAGES OF CABBERS	
Able to perform some operations that flat laps can't, such as concave shapes like hearts or moons (although this involves a more advanced technique)	
More efficient when doing individual pieces one at a time since you don't have to stop and swap the individual grinding, sanding, and polishing discs; if you are doing pieces in groups, there's minimal efficiency gain.	

pieces or stones you can work with. That said, if you're only going to be making jewelry pieces or cabochons, the 6-inch machine might suffice.

PURCHASING A CABOCHON MAKING AND FACE-POLISHING MACHINE

Hi-Tech Diamond 8-inch flat lapidary grinder-polisher

RICHARD PAUPORE

Flat Laps and Slant Laps

Through many years of intensive testing and use, we've found the Hi-Tech Diamond flat lap and slant lap machines to be more durable and sturdy than other brands, like Ameritool, which is a high-quality machine. Furthermore, the Hi-Tech machines are more accepting of replacement discs made by removing and replacing the top plates that are attached to the original backer plates (see tip below).

HELPFUL TIP For flat lap discs, you can replace just the top plates that are attached to the thicker backer plates (see page 114 for details on how to do this). At press time, replacing just the top plates for a set of five discs was about $160, whereas a full set of new discs with backer plates was $410, for a savings of $250.

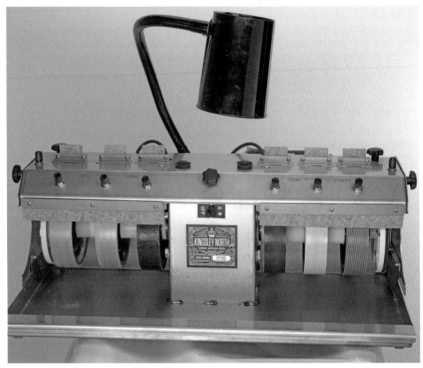

Kingsley North KNC6 6-inch cabber   RICHARD PAUPORE

The choice of flat lap vs. slant lap boils down to personal preference and is really one of ergonomics. With a flat lap, you need to tilt your head to the left or right (depending on which side of the disc you normally work on) to observe the work you are doing. With the slant lap, the surface of the disc will be tilted up and toward you, so there's less strain on your head and neck. Otherwise, the slant lap machine comes with all the same accessories, uses the same discs, and follows the same processes as the flat lap.

Cabber Machines

As with the flat laps, we recommend cabbers that have proven their reliability and performance over many years. Because of its valuable innovations developed through extensive investment in research, our top recommendation is the Kingsley North KNC6. Some of the key features of its latest model include more space between wheels, individual shutoff valves for each wheel, top-mounted lubrication ports with easy-to-remove plastic caps, a stainless steel chassis, an additional felt strip for better water distribution, felt strips that are easier to remove/replace, and side discs that can be used with the shields/door in place. The CabKing 6-inch and Diamond Pacific Genie 6-inch are also high-quality machines and excellent choices for both beginning and advanced hobbyists.

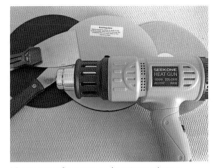

Submersible water pump and hoses   Heat gun for removing top plates

Flat Lap and Cabber Supplies

Flat laps use a series of grinding, sanding, and polishing discs (cabbers use vertical wheels) to remove material from a gemstone. We will primarily refer to discs below, but the information can also be applied to wheels if you're using a cabber. Each successive disc is finer and less abrasive, so each produces more of a sanding, smoothing, or polishing effect than the one before it.

We will describe the different types of discs in the order they are used. We list the most commonly available colors for the given type of disc; however, disc colors can change, so the most important thing to understand is the numerical mesh of the grinding materials on the surface of the disc.

1. **Coarse grinding disc (100 mesh) or wheel (80 mesh) (optional).** A silver metal-bonded disc with very coarse diamond abrasives. This disc should be used with care, as it can cause deep grooves and scratches in a stone. This ultracoarse disc is needed only when there's a large amount of material to be removed, such as when face-polishing a large stone with major surface flaws.

2. **Standard grinding disc (180 mesh) or wheel (220 mesh).** A silver metal-bonded disc with coarse diamond abrasives. This disc will be your workhorse for chamfering and doming smaller stones and cabochons. And if you've used a coarse grinding disc on a stone, this grinding disc will be used to remove the deeper scratches made by the coarse grind. It is a close equivalent to the coarse abrasive/grit used in the first stage of tumble-polishing.

3. **Sanding disc (325 mesh) or wheel (280 mesh).** A resin-bonded disc or wheel that is used to remove surface scratches and grooves caused by the grinding discs; it is also used to finely contour the gemstone surface.

4. **Smoothing disc (600 mesh) or wheel (1,200 mesh).** Resin-bonded discs or wheels that are covered with diamond abrasives. These discs remove tiny residual scratches, perform surface smoothing, and ultimately prepare the surface of the stones for polishing. Note that additional smoothing discs

can be used in sequence, but they are truly for ultrahigh-grade stones that warrant the extra time and investment to obtain superglossy finishes. In most cases, these discs aren't required.

5. **Polishing disc or wheel.** For flat laps, you can use a white absorbent felt disc to apply polishing paste to gemstones, creating a high-gloss finish. Alternatively, you can use a 360-mesh diamond polishing disc precharged with cerium oxide, which is also used with some cabbers and is exposed at one end of the machine for full face use.

6. **Polishing paste.** There are various gradients of diamond polishing paste, but a single 14,000-mesh gradient is usually sufficient. The polishing paste itself consists of small diamond particles.

7. **Coolants/lubricants.** Flat laps and cabbers require coolants, which also serve as lubricants. The machines we recommend use water, which is supplied through a small plastic feeder tube. For flat laps, this tube is connected to a cup that sits above the sanding surface; for cabbers, the tube is attached to a pump that is immersed in a large bucket or tub of water. Excess water drains out through another plastic tube into a small cup or tray, but we recommend attaching a flexible hose to the machines that feeds directly into a separate bucket to avoid having to monitor and periodically empty your cup or tray.

Additional Supplies

There are many other supplies that will make you more proficient and productive. Some of the most important are pictured. Besides those, you will need **mineral oil** to cure fractures and **acetone** to remove cabochons from bolts; **safety goggles, an N95 or KN95 mask, and hearing protection;** and **a bucket, a 3-foot-long plastic drainage hose,** and (if you will be working standing up) **a cushioned floor mat.**

HELPFUL TIP Like diamond saw blades, the abrasive materials that coat grinding, sanding, and polishing discs eventually wear down and need to be replaced. You can obtain many hours of use from them and produce a large quantity of beautiful display specimens before needing to replace them. The notable exception is if you are primarily face-polishing large stones that need a lot of grinding and shaping.

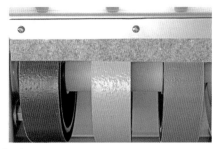

6-inch cabber wheel set   RICHARD PAUPORE

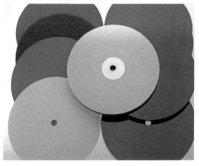

8-inch flat lap disc set
RICHARD PAUPORE

Submersible water pump
(for cabbers)   RICHARD PAUPORE

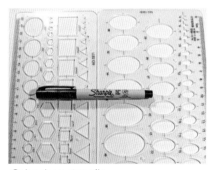

Cabochon stencils

Dish rack for storing discs

Krazy Glue and bolts

Self-adhesive veterinary tape

85

Rubber washers for discs with thinner backer plates

2-inch plastic spring clamps to hold flat lap splash guard in place

5x lighted magnifier for inspection

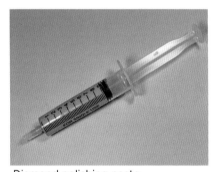

Diamond polishing paste

SETUP AND OPERATION

SAFETY

Never grind or sand your stones without water dripping onto the disc (but don't use water with the polishing disc, as this will ruin the disc). Use of lubricants saves wear and tear on the discs, produces better results, and is the most important way to minimize your chances of developing silicosis (see note on page 8). This is especially important when you're working with any toxic gemstone materials like malachite. While you don't sand or grind with the polishing disc, it does produce microscopic diamond particles. Therefore, whether you're grinding, sanding, or polishing, we recommend having a good ventilating fan and wearing an N95 or KN95 mask or respirator to further reduce the possibility of inhaling either rock dust or diamond particles.

Whereas saw blades are relatively safe, metal-bonded coarse and fine grinding discs and wheels can quickly grind away skin and fingernails and hence require a greater degree of caution than lapidary saws. This is why we recommend that beginners especially not work with stones much smaller than golf ball size and when working with jewelry pieces to ensure they are attached to a bolt head or nail spike. These precautions will keep your fingertips a safe distance above the grinding surface. Additionally, you can use self-adhesive veterinary tape to protect your finger tips (see page 85).

Additionally, we recommend that you wear safety goggles when using the coarse or standard grinding discs or the coarse sanding disk.

FLAT LAP SETUP

The flat lap makes little or no mess. Setup is quite simple since the machine comes with a water-supply cup and a drainage cup. We suggest purchasing a 3-foot-long plastic hose that you can attach to your machine and run into a 5-gallon bucket so that you don't have to continually empty the drainage cup. In terms of your workspace, it's a good idea to set up your face-polishing work-station in an area where the noise won't carry into other areas of your home, and where you are OK with a small amount of rock dust getting onto things in the immediate vicinity.

In addition, as you go through the sequential grinding, sanding, and polishing stages, you'll be inspecting your gemstones often, so your work area should be well lit, with an adjustable desk lamp at your workstation. A dish rack and a small hand towel are helpful, as they will help you store your grinding, sanding, and polishing discs; keeping your discs in an upright position allows them to dry between uses and maximizes their product life. Lay the towel over the top of your discs when you are finished working to prevent dust (or oil spray from your rock saw) from falling on them and decreasing their useful life. Finally, if you set up your machine so that you will be working standing up, you should have durable cushioned floor mats.

CABBER SETUP

Your cabber will also require a submersible pump. The Kingsley North KNC6 machine will otherwise require minimal setup once you've assembled all the components that come with it. Follow the setup recommendations for the flat lap as far as the location of your workstation. Cabbers are much heavier than flat laps, so you'll also need a sturdy workbench.

FLAT LAP OPERATION

Before you start, always fill the water-supply cup to the top and ensure that the drainage tube is emptying into a water cup or your 5-gallon bucket. (*Note:* Never start the water drip until the disc is mounted and the machine is running; if water drips down the shaft where the discs are bolted on, it can ruin the motor.) Next, place the appropriate disc onto the flat lap. To do so, simply unscrew the top bolt, place your disc on the spindle, and tighten the top bolt. The thickness of the backing plates varies; you'll need a rubber washer for the thinner discs.

Now you're ready to start the machine. The flat lap we recommend is controlled through a variable-speed dial on the front of the machine, making it incredibly easy to operate. Most of the time, we recommend running the machine at full speed, as this will achieve the desired results more quickly, and it allows you to apply the maximum amount of pressure without slowing the rotation speed of the disc, which can result in additional abrasions or flat spots on the stone's surface.

Once the disc is spinning, turn the small knob on the water-supply tube until water is dripping at about two drops per second. The end of the water-supply tube should be about even with where the grinding abrasive begins at the center of the disc. The entire surface of the disc should become damp. You will need to periodically refill the water-supply cup and empty the drainage cup if you aren't draining into a 5-gallon bucket. Before turning the machine off, make sure the water drip has been completely stopped and you've turned the drip nozzle away from the disc to avoid getting water down the shaft.

CABBER OPERATION

Submerge the pump in a 5-gallon bucket of water that is at least half full. Once you turn the machine on, all the wheels will start to spin. With the cabbers we recommend, there are separate water-drip dials for each wheel; just turn them on or off as you progress through the sequence of grinding, sanding, and polishing your pieces.

CABOCHON MAKING AND FACE-POLISHING STEP-BY-STEP

As mentioned, there is a large amount of overlap in the steps and detailed processes for cabochon making and face-polishing. As we go through the details for each process, we'll call out any differences between the two, but there will be more emphasis on cabochon making. Therefore, we'll provide additional details for things that are unique to face-polishing after going through the shared process steps.

There are a few different cabochon types and setting options that will affect the steps below. Some of the most common options are described here, along with their process variations.

1. **Natural-shape cabochons** are perhaps the simplest type to make. You start by cutting slabs or slices from a whole stone, generally agates. After that, if you don't want to dome the top surface, you can either grind the front and back surfaces with the standard 180-mesh disc or 220-mesh wheel to remove any saw marks. If you want to dome the top surface, you should skip

CABOCHON MAKING AND FACE-POLISHING REFERENCE

STEP	NATURAL-SHAPE CABOCHON	SHAPED CABOCHON	FACE-POLISHED STONE
1. Stencil shape onto slab.	No	Yes	No
2. Cut to rough shape.	No	Yes	No
3. Clean stone.	Yes	Yes	Yes
4. Grind to stencil outline.	No	Yes	No
5. Sand and fine-sand front and back sides.	Yes	Back side only	No
6.* Attach stone to bolt or nail spike.	No	Yes	No
7. Chamfer, dome, smooth, and sand the stone.	No	Yes	Yes
8. Remove cabochon from bolt or nail.	No	Yes	No
9. Tumble-polish.	Yes	Optional	Optional
10. Apply mineral oil to cure fractures.	Optional	Optional	Optional

* The bolt can be attached either before or after creating the chamfer.

the chamfering step and just start with the inward sweeping and rotational grinding actions while taking care not to grind away the outer edges of the slab. Once you have a nicely domed surface, you should also grind the back surface smooth. Next, you can finish your piece(s) in your tumbler. Otherwise, you can go through the full set of discs (or wheels) on both surfaces of the stone. The latter method is more labor-intensive and won't give as consistent a polish, but if you have only a few pieces, it's much faster.

2. **Shaped cabochons,** with no doming of the top surface, are similar to natural-shape cabochons except that you first stencil, trim, and shape your pieces on the saw and grinder. After that, you grind both surfaces smooth and either finish with the complete series of discs or wheels or finish in your tumbler.

3. **Cabochons fitted to a standard-size bezel cup** is the same as making shaped cabochons with a stencil to make oval, round, or other symmetrically shaped pieces. There are numerous makers of high-quality bezel cups, or blanks, that are pure silver, silver plated, stainless steel, gold, and other metals. We'll talk about these options more in Chapter 8. The increased difficulty of making fitted cabochons is the high degree of precision needed to ensure a tight fit all around the rim of the bezel cup so that there aren't unpleasing gaps

between the stone and the rim. Like drilling, it will take considerable patience and practice to master this skill.

With face-polishing, you can create stones with either a domed (rounded) surface or a flat surface. We'll primarily focus on creating domed surfaces since it's far easier to get a consistent high-gloss finish across the polished face.

The table on page 89 shows the linear steps and whether they are applicable based on what you are creating. As you can see, shaped cabochons are the most labor-intensive, whereas natural-shape cabochons are the least. Step 7 is high-lighted since it has multiple substeps, or stages, and is the core of the process for both cabochon making and face-polishing.

STEP 1: STENCIL SHAPE ONTO SLAB (shaped cabochons only)

This step assumes that you've created or acquired rough gemstone slabs large enough to create one or more cabochons using your chosen stencil outline.

First, determine which side of your gemstone slab will be the top side of your finished cabochons (while some cabochons are finished on both sides, most usually display only one side, which we will refer to as the top side). With the top side face-up, identify a section of your slab that has pleasing colors and patterns. Place your stencil over the area you've identified and move it around until you find a sweet spot. Before beginning to mark the outline, consider whether you will use the slab to make multiple cabochons. If so, you might draw some light outlines with a regular graphite pencil and then move the template around to see whether you have enough space for a second shape. In general, you should leave at least ¼ inch between your stenciled shapes.

Use a fine-point permanent marker to mark the outline on the slab. Angle the point of the marker outward to ensure the stencil shape is marked cleanly.

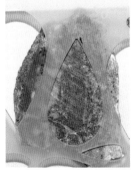
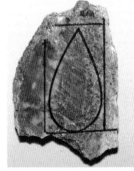

A copper slab to be shaped using a cabber

A lapis lazuli slab to be shaped using a flat lap

Next, use a ruler or straightedge to mark a rectangular pattern that is approximately ⅛ inch outside of the borders of the stenciled shape. You could also use a square or rectangle stencil shape to draw this border. The border will be your cut lines for trim-sawing. It's best to extend the lines of these patterns past the corners somewhat with a ruler to help line up your trim-saw blade and make nice square cuts.

HELPFUL TIP We recommend that beginners start with basic shapes, such as those available on the templates shown on page 85. As your skills improve, we also encourage you to explore your creative instincts by designing your own patterns. Some of the most beautiful cabochons are free-form, meaning they have been styled on the fly after starting with a general design pattern. Your love for making cabs will grow over time as you develop your own unique patterns.

STEP 2: CUT TO ROUGH SHAPE
(shaped cabochons only)

Using a trim saw, cut along the rectangular border. To reduce the amount of wasted gemstone material, cut as close to the stenciled lines as possible. Since you are cutting from a flat slab, you won't need to use the rocking-and-rolling technique described on page 74, but you should still reduce the amount of pressure against the saw blade as you get to the edge of the slab.

After you've cut along the lines you drew, there might still be a significant amount of excess material that should be sawed off (rather than ground off); this not only saves time but also reduces wear on your

Lapis slab with excess trimmed

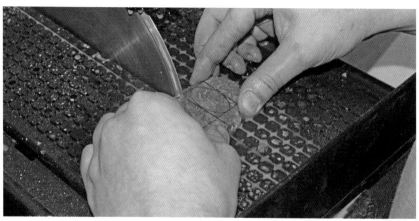

Trimming along the "cut lines" of the stenciled copper slab

grinding discs or wheels. However, you should not cut closer than ⅛ inch to the stencil outline.

STEP 3: CLEAN THE STONE (all cabochons)

Clean the cabochon thoroughly to ensure it adheres firmly to the bolt or nail in Step 6. Use a strong degreasing dishwashing liquid, such as Dawn or Ajax.

STEP 4: GRIND TO STENCIL SHAPE (shaped cabochons only)

Mount your coarse/rough grinding disc on the flat lap, turn the machine on, and start the water dripping, as described on pages 87–88.

Press the edge of the rough cabochon against the disc and gradually rotate the stone all the way around, grinding right up to the stenciled outline.

Take a final "lap" around the circumference of the stone until all the excess material has been removed and the stencil outline is no longer visible.

Coarse-grinding copper piece to stenciled outline

After coarse-grinding

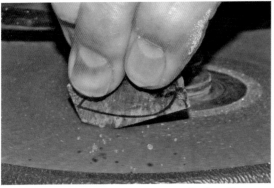
Coarse-grinding lapis piece to stenciled outline
DIANE MAGNUSON

After coarse-grinding

STEP 5: SAND AND FINE-SAND THE FRONT AND BACK
(back side only for shaped cabochons)

Using your standard 180-mesh disc or 325-mesh sanding disc, sand away any noticeable saw marks from the back side of your shaped cabochons and natural-shape cabochons. For your natural-shape cabs, flip them over and do the same on the front sides.

If you don't plan to tumble-polish your shaped cabs, use the 600-mesh fine-sanding disc to give them a soft glow on the back side. If you plan to tumble-polish them, skip this step. If you plan to tumble-polish your natural-shape cabs (which is what we recommend), you can skip this step as well.

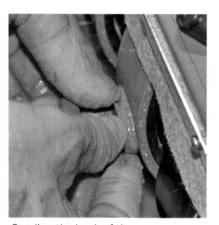

Sanding the back of the copper cabochon

Sanding the back of the lapis cabochon   DIANE MAGNUSON

STEP 6: ATTACH TO BOLT OR SPIKE NAIL
(shaped cabochons only)

Put a small drop of Krazy Glue (or a similar fast-drying adhesive), and then press the head of the bolt or nail spike onto the stone and hold it steady for 30–60 seconds. Let stand 5 minutes to allow the glue to dry fully. We recommend using flat-head bolts rather than nail spikes because the threads on the bolt allow you to grip it more securely. If you use a nail spike, make sure to grind the spike flat to avoid getting poked. (Note that we used to recommend a process known as dopping, but it's a significantly more complex and messy process that requires an additional machine and special supplies.) Once you have the piece on a bolt, you can either hold the bolt about midway on the threaded portion, or position your thumb and first two fingers at the base of the bolt, so that they are flat against the bottom of the cabochon. You'll see examples of both in the photos for the lapis cabochon. The latter method gives you a little better feel for how the piece is being shaped or sanded by the discs.

| Adding glue to back of lapis cabochon | Bolt glued to lapis cabochon |

Finally, some hobbyists like to use veterinary self-adhesive tape/bandage wrap on their fingers to protect against scrapes and abrasions, and then optionally put the cabochon onto a bolt or nail head.

STEP 7: CHAMFERING, DOMING, SMOOTHING, AND SANDING (shaped cabochons and face-polished stones only)

This is the core of the process for both cabochon making and face-polishing, and it includes multiple substeps, or stages. Before describing the process details, we provide an overview to inspecting your work, along with a handy reference guide, below. All of the subsequent process details refer to discs that are used on flat laps. The steps and process details are the same for cabbers except that you are using wheels, some of which have different mesh ratings than their corresponding discs. These differences are reflected in the reference guide.

Inspecting Your Work

As mentioned earlier, you can turn out nicely polished cabochons and stones in 15–30 minutes. But if you rush from stage to stage, you will get to the end and

POLISHING STAGES QUICK GUIDE

STAGE	FLAT LAP DISC	FLAT LAP DISC MESH	DISC COLOR
1	Coarse-grinding (optional)	100	Silver
1	Standard grinding	180	Silver
2	Sanding	325	Brown
3	Smoothing	600	Red
3	Prepolishing	1,200	Blue
3	Prepolishing (optional)	3,000	Orange
4	Polishing	14,000 or cerium-charged	White

wonder why your stones have only a dull glow instead of the high-gloss shine you expected. Therefore, a good inspection is the secret to cabochon making and face-polishing. After you finish a stage in the process, it's time to clean your gemstones; stop and take a look at your work; and, if necessary, revisit that step. To clean your pieces, dip them in your water-supply cup and rub them gently with a soft rag to remove any grit or ground rock. Then give them a moment to air-dry so there is no remaining moisture, which can mask small imperfections.

When it comes to these inspections, we cannot overemphasize the importance of attention to detail; inspections enable you to check your work, thereby avoiding having to return to previous stages or discs and ensuring a higher-quality result. To make things easier for you, we provide inspection tips at the end of each stage, plus a handy visual guide starting on page 108.

Stage 1: Chamfering, Doming, and Smoothing

These processes involve removing material starting at the edges of your cabochon or stone and moving toward the center such that the center becomes the highest point of the dome. The steeper you want the dome to be, the more material you'll need to remove. The graphic on the following page illustrates this concept for a round or circular cabochon.

CHAMFERING

The first step in doming or contouring a cabochon or stone is to create a beveled edge around the face of the entire stone; this is called a **chamfer.** You should do this for stones even if they weren't trim-cut first. For cabochons that need a lot of material removed and for larger stones or stones with deeper surface indentations, more material will need to be removed. In this case, you might want to start with the coarse (100-mesh) grinding disc, and you need to create a chamfer

CABBER WHEEL MESH	WHEEL COLOR	STEP IS COMPLETE WHEN
80	Silver	The piece is the shape you want.
220	Silver	The piece is smooth and nicely contoured.
280	Black	There are no visible scratch marks.
600	Burgundy	There is a faint glow.
1,200	Vanilla	There is a semigloss glow.
3,000	Pink	There is a glossy shine.
Felt or cerium-charged	White	There is a high-gloss shine.

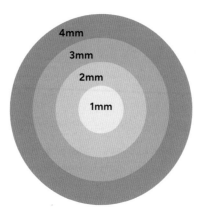

If your cabochon (or stone) is perfectly round, you might reduce material incrementally, removing 4 millimeters from the outer circle, 3 millimeters from the next circle, 2 millimeters from the next, and 1 millimeter from the inner circle.

that is wider and more steeply angled, say at a 45-degree angle to the face. For smaller stones and cabochons, the chamfer will be relatively narrow and at a lower angle, say 30 degrees, and we recommend using the standard (180-mesh) grinding disc, which also produces less pronounced scratches that will later need to be sanded away. In general, we recommend creating a **secondary chamfer** starting at the inner edge of the **initial chamfer.**

To create the chamfer, place the edge of the face of the stone against the grinding disc at the desired angle and slowly rotate the stone. Work all the way around the stone until you have a uniform bevel. For larger cabochons and stones, you can repeat this process two to three times to create a wide or layered chamfer. These larger pieces also require a more pronounced chamfer angle. You might prefer to perform the chamfering step before attaching the piece to a bolt, as it's a little easier to get at the edge of the stone while working it. This is how we did this step for the lapis piece as seen in the photo on the opposite page, above right.

You're finished when you have a chamfer that is wide and deep enough that by the time the stone is smoothly domed from the center of the face to the chamfered edge, all surface-depth variations and flaws have been removed.

HELPFUL TIP Larger cabochons and gemstones need a deeper and wider chamfer, and usually a secondary chamfer. This is where the coarse grinding disc really comes in handy, as it quickly removes more stone and shapes highly uneven surfaces quickly and efficiently. When using the coarse disc, be careful not to apply too much pressure; that will leave deeper scratches in your stones that require a lot of grinding and sanding to smooth over.

Chamfering the copper cabochon

Chamfering the lapis cabochon

DIANE MAGNUSON

DOMING

After creating the chamfer, begin to work your gemstone into a smooth, domed shape. It's critical to always be moving the stone when it's in contact with the disc to reduce deep scratch marks and flat spots, or **facets.**

Begin by pressing the outer edge of the stone against the disc and making inward sweeping motions while also applying significant pressure against the grinding disc. Apply more pressure on the outer edge of the stone to remove more material, and less pressure as you sweep inward to remove less material toward the center of the stone. You can exert quite a lot of force without slowing the speed of the disc, and as long as you're moving the cabochon or stone, you won't damage

Doming the lapis cabochon   DIANE MAGNUSON

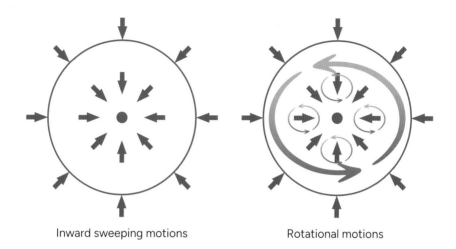

Inward sweeping motions   Rotational motions

it. Then, gradually rotate the piece clockwise or counterclockwise and perform the same inward sweeping motions from multiple angles around the circumference of the stone (see illustration above left). As the surface becomes smoother and dome-shaped, begin to introduce circular rotation in small, focused areas of the surface and then around the entire surface (see illustration above right). As you perform these movements, try to envision the surface shape you are trying to create, and feel with your fingertips how the stone is engaging the disc; we like to call this "thinking in 3D." These motions taken together will result in a symmetrical, smooth dome that rises toward the center point.

SMOOTHING

If you've been using the coarse disc, you should now switch to the standard grinding disc to smooth out some of the heavier scratches made by the coarse disc. Repeat the same inward sweeping and rotational motions across the entire domed surface one or two times, and then inspect your work to ensure you have removed any deep scratches or grooves. This activity will also remove most of the flat spots and angular faceting, so that the surface is smooth and nicely rounded.

Finally, you need to round out the top and bottom edges of the cabochon all the way around the perimeter. This is especially important if you won't be finishing your cabochons in a tumbler. You'll perform this rounding by placing the top edge of the cabochon against the disc at a slight tilt and performing a rocking motion between the bottom and top edges all the way around the perimeter. Note that you also need to perform this edge-rounding action for all of the subsequent discs (sanding, fine-sanding, prepolish, and polish), unless you finish your cabochons in a tumbler.

You're finished with this stage when your whole stone or cabochon has a nicely contoured dome shape and no significant surface indentations are visible to the naked eye (any indentations should be less than 0.5 millimeter deep). The surface of the stone will be scratchy and rough, but this isn't a concern; subsequent sanding and smoothing operations will remove the scratches and minor surface flaws.

HELPFUL TIP There are some softer materials, such as lapis lazuli, that require less force than harder stones like agates and jaspers, so take this into consideration as you polish different types of gemstone materials. In fact, we recommend not using the coarse grinding disc with these softer materials. Instead, use the standard grinding disc in its place.

CHECKING YOUR WORK

Chamfering You're finished when the piece exhibits a uniform chamfer (beveled edge) around the circumference of the stone; it might be a **layered chamfer** if you created successive chamfers on larger pieces where you want a more pronounced dome.

Chamfered, domed lapis cabochon

Doming You're finished when the surface is uniformly rounded and smooth and no pits or surface-depth variations greater than 0.5 millimeters deep remain; you will have a nicely contoured surface that follows the outline of the stone and gently rises to a dome toward the middle of the stone's surface. The surface will be visibly rough when dry, with noticeable scratches.

Smoothing You're finished when the surface is uniformly smooth but dull and a bit scratchy in spots. The surface will be nicely rounded with minimal flat spots, or facets.

Stage 2: Coarse-Sanding

Coarse-sanding removes only a small amount of material (except with softer gemstones), so before beginning this stage, make sure you've reduced the stone down to the shape and surface contour you want your finished piece to have. The sanding disc removes any remaining sharp edges or angles left from rough-grinding and removes all scratches that are visible to the naked eye.

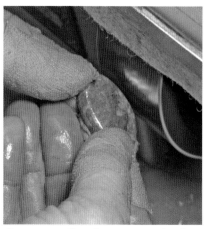

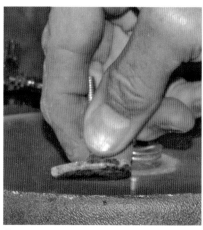

Coarse-sanding the copper cabochon   Coarse-sanding the lapis cabochon

DIANE MAGNUSON

Use the same techniques as in the doming stage by placing the outer edge against the disc, making inward and upward sweeping motions and rotational motions while gradually rotating the stone clockwise or counterclockwise. Be sure to move around the entire surface of the stone. Pay extra attention to the outer edges of the stone, as this is where some of the heavier grinding was performed, and you should work to round off any sharp edges all around the surface.

Cleaning, thoroughly drying, and inspecting your gemstones is very important during the sanding stage, as *this is your last chance to remove any significant scratches and flaws left in the stone.* You will probably do this two to three times. This helps you ensure your gemstone has a uniform surface texture that is smooth and nicely contoured.

CHECKING YOUR WORK

You're finished when there are no abrasions or scratches; the stones have a smooth, uniform surface and even the hint of a soft glow; and there are no pits or surface-depth variations visible to the naked eye. (When we say no pits or dimples, we mean zero! Otherwise, they will show up as dull spots on your polished gemstones and cabochons.) The edges of the stone must be smoothed in with the overall surface, with no flat spots or sharp edges.

If you have not achieved these results, either go back to the standard grinding

Coarse-sanded lapis cabochon

disc to remove the flaws or continue with the sanding operation until you get to the desired outcome. Whatever you do, don't skip ahead to the next stage; this will only waste your time and you'll have to circle back through the last several stages a second time.

Note: At this point, you might decide to finish your pieces in a tumbler. If so, skip to Step 9 (page 104).

Stage 3: Fine-Sanding and Prepolishing

The fine-sanding and prepolishing discs prepare the domed surface of the cabochon or stone for polishing. No gemstone material will be removed by either of these discs unless you're working with very soft materials, such as those with a hardness rating of 5 or below. Use the same process as described for stage 2 and make sure to move around the entire surface of the piece while continuing to exert significant pressure of the stone against the discs. Each of these discs should take about half the time that was required for coarse-sanding.

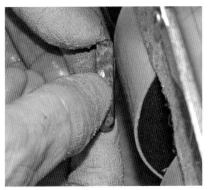

Fine-sanding the copper cabochon

Fine-sanding the lapis cabochon
DIANE MAGNUSON

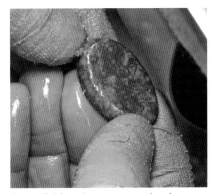

Prepolishing the copper cabochon

Prepolishing the lapis cabochon
DIANE MAGNUSON

You're finished when the stones have a uniformly smooth surface, a soft glow across the entire face or dome, and no dull or slightly scratchy spots.

Lapis cabochon after fine-sanding

Lapis cabochon after prepolishing

Copper cabochon after prepolishing. The prepolish brought this piece to full polish, so no further polishing is needed.

HELPFUL TIP When you first get started with cabochon making and face-polishing, you might be inclined to rush this stage, but resist the temptation because this last step is what sets you up for a killer high-gloss shine vs. a nice but subpar polish.

Stage 4: Polishing

Polishing is the last stage in the face-polishing process. Whereas all previous stages are about removing material, shaping the stone, and preparing its surface for polishing, this stage adds something: the specialized polishing compounds that give your gemstone that high-gloss shine.

Polishing the lapis cabochon   DIANE MAGNUSON

To polish a cabochon or stone, you first need to attach the polishing disc; you can use either a felt-covered disc or a cerium-charged disc (note that water is not used with felt discs, so *be sure to have your water drip turned off before you start*). For felt discs, instead of using water, inject three or four small streaks of diamond polishing compound onto the disc using the injection tube. This amount will last for several pieces, depending on their size. Use your forefinger to lightly spread the paste onto the disc; it will not cover the entire surface of the disc. If using a cerium-charged polishing disc, *note that you will use a water drip, without paste,* just as you do for all of the other discs.

Now it's time to start polishing. Start the machine and hold the stone against the disc. You don't need to exert as much pressure when polishing; if you use too much, polishing compound will come off the disc too quickly. *Be sure to have an extra-firm grip on the stone if using a felt polishing disc;* because you aren't using water, the disc will tend to grab the stone and pull it from your hand. When polishing, use the same motions as the prior stages, gradually rotating the stone clockwise or counterclockwise while also rocking it, moving around its entire surface.

After you've polished the entire surface, use a soft cloth to gently rub away excess polishing compound and buff the cabochon or stone. Polishing takes less than a minute, much less

Fully polished lapis cabochon

than the previous stages. If you aren't getting a high-gloss shine, do another full polish. If it's still not satisfactory, you might need to repeat prior stages.

CHECKING YOUR WORK

You're finished when you look at your pieces and they look back at you and smile! We really mean it: There is no second-guessing the beaming shine that tells you, "That's a job well done!" The gemstones should have a consistent high-gloss polish and no dull or uneven spots.

STEP 8: REMOVE CABOCHON FROM BOLT OR NAIL

Fill a small glass jar with acetone; immerse the stone and bolt in acetone, then close the jar. We recommend letting the pieces sit in the acetone bath for 12

hours so that the cabochon comes off without the use of a razor blade. If you are pressed for time, you should allow your pieces to soak for at least 30 minutes, then use a razor blade to slide between the cabochon and bolt head to loosen and remove it. Scrape off any excess glue with the razor blade once the cabochon comes free.

STEP 9: TUMBLE-POLISHING (OPTIONAL)

Soaking the piece in acetone to loosen the glue

You might wish to fully (or partially) polish your cabochons or stones after you complete stage 2, coarse-sanding. Usually this is done for efficiency, but it can also give you a smoother and more consistent finish. In fact, most experienced lapidary artists use a tumbler for the final polishing steps of cabochon making. If you have 10 or more cabochons, you'll get more done with less effort by using the tumbler. Other benefits of the tumbler are that it polishes both sides of the cabochon and does a nice job of creating smooth, naturally rounded edges.

- For cabochons, this means you'll perform all of the fine-sanding and polishing in the tumbler.

- For face-polished stones, you might just run them through medium grit in the tumbler and then perform the prepolish and polishing steps on the flat lap or cabber; this depends on whether you want the whole stone to be polished or only the main face.

STEP 10: APPLY MINERAL OIL TO CURE FRACTURES

Many gemstones have hidden fractures that emerge while performing lapidary work. A simple way to minimize or even completely eliminate the appearance of these flaws is to apply a coating of mineral oil and let it soak into the stone for several days before buffing dry.

FACE-POLISHING OPTIONS AND CONSIDERATIONS

In addition to the detailed process instructions provided thus far, there are a few options and special considerations for face-polishing.

DOMED SURFACES VS. FLAT SURFACES

When face-polishing, you need to decide whether you want your polished surface to be domed or flat. With a domed surface, it is far easier to obtain a uniform high-gloss polish. That's because a curved area exposes less surface area to the disc at a time; this allows you to apply more pressure to that area. In fact, if you're polishing a curved surface, you can apply up to 10 times as much pressure as you could to a flat surface, helping to remove even small dimples.

From a practical standpoint, it's quite difficult to get a uniform finish with flat face-polishing, and it will consume much more of the diamond coating on the discs or wheels. Therefore, the bulk of our discussion will focus on creating dome-polished surfaces. If you intend to polish a lot of stones with flat surfaces, you're best to go with a **vibrating lapidary machine,** which is made solely for polishing flat-surface gemstones. We don't cover those machines in this book because they are considerably more expensive and are considered a more advanced application.

CHOOSING THE RIGHT GEMSTONES TO FACE-POLISH

Before you start polishing, you need to choose the right gemstones. There are two types of stones you can face-polish. One option is to start with a whole or rough stone that has a reasonably even surface and some nice color and pattern exposed; a stone with an even and slightly rounded surface is a great fit because you don't need to do an excessive amount of grinding.

You can also face-polish whole stones that either lack a visible pattern or stones that have major surface flaws, but before you can polish these stones, you might need to cut them using a lapidary saw.

CHOOSING WHOLE STONES

Let's talk about whole stones first—whole stones are simply natural stones that have not been cut using a lapidary saw. While you can achieve a nicely curved dome when starting with a flat stone, with a whole stone you can achieve this doming effect faster because you won't need to cut the stone first and there's usually less material to grind away. Dome-polishing a whole stone is easiest if the stone has the following features:

- **Exposed surface colors and patterns** If you cannot readily see the color and pattern on a stone, you will spend too much time grinding away the rough outer surface. Such stones may be good candidates for **face-cutting** (cutting off a portion of the stone to remove flaws or expose more pattern) or simply cutting into equal halves. Either way, cutting is done with a lapidary saw and results in a flat surface that can then be domed, ground, and polished.

- **Minimal depth variation** If more than 5 millimeters of stone needs to be ground away to obtain a smooth surface (from the outer edge to the center point), you'll spend much more time grinding than you probably have the patience for. This will also wear out your discs more quickly. Stones with jagged points or deep pits are good candidates for face-cutting, then shaping and polishing.

- **Absence of deep fractures** Even though a stone may have a reasonably flat or nicely contoured surface with nice colors and patterns, it might contain surface fractures that could go deeper into the stone. If a stone has a fracture that appears to extend beneath the surface of the stone, wet the stone and shine a bright light on it. If the fracture appears to go deep into the stone, cutting it might be worthwhile, though it's possible the stone is worthless for lapidary purposes if the fracture(s) spoils the beauty of the stone.

CUTTING STONES FOR FACE-POLISHING

When you are cutting stones for face-polishing, it's critical that you follow all the tips in Chapter 4 (pages 70–76). Following those tips will substantially minimize the extra grinding that would be needed to get a perfectly polished face. Regardless of how clean your saw cut is, for face-cut stones you will almost always use the chamfering technique described on pages 95–96 to bring the surface to a dome shape; this will also remove saw cut marks and dimples.

HELPFUL TIP When using the machines recommended in this book, you shouldn't try to face-polish stones more than 3 inches in diameter.

DETERMINING HOW TO FACE-POLISH A STONE

In some ways, face-polishing gemstones is similar to cutting them. When face-polishing, you need to select the surface you want to polish and how best to approach it. As with cutting, this is somewhat intuitive, which means there is no perfect way to decide how to orient your gemstone on the grinding disc. Just as with cutting, when you first get started face-polishing, it's a good idea to practice on lower-quality materials before starting to polish higher-grade gemstones. It's also a good idea to learn on smaller stones (1–2 inches in diameter). This will get you comfortable with using the machine and will help you practice important operations, such as initiating the grinding operation and rocking, rotating, and sanding the stone. Below are some general guidelines to help determine the best polishing surface and angle for your gemstones.

MAXIMIZE THE MOST BEAUTIFUL FEATURES

Look for the most striking color or pattern combinations that are already exposed on the stone, but also take into consideration areas that would require extensive grinding.

BRING THE SURFACE TO AN EVEN LEVEL AND REMOVE FLAWS

If the gemstone you want to face-polish has an uneven surface or significant surface flaws or blemishes, the first thing you need to do is address these issues. Protruding material needs to be ground away to make a nearly even surface. Grooves, pits, and valleys are removed by grinding away the excess surface material surrounding them. (If there is more than 5 millimeters of material to remove, it's better to face-cut the stone than try to grind away that much material.) Once you have achieved a nearly even surface, or if you started with a stone that was already face-cut, you can start to create a domed or contoured surface.

HOW TO HOLD AND MOVE YOUR GEMSTONES

Because of the previously mentioned safety concerns (especially with metal-bonded grinding discs), it's important to have a firm grip on the stone before beginning your work. Also, unlike with cabochon making, you won't be attaching your stones to a bolt or nail head. We suggest that you use your thumb and first three fingers to hold the stone securely. Also, hold the stone such that there is at least 5 millimeters of clearance between the tips of your fingers and the surface of the discs.

FACE-POLISHING VISUAL GUIDE

A rough Lake Superior agate to be face-polished on a cabber

A rough Purple Passion agate to be face-polished on a flat lap
DIANE MAGNUSON

STEP 1: CREATE CHAMFER AROUND RIM OF STONE
(not necessary on the Lake Superior agate because the surface was already nicely contoured)

Chamfering the Purple Passion agate   DIANE MAGNUSON

Purple Passion agate with chamfer   DIANE MAGNUSON

STEP 2: CREATE DOME (COARSE-GRIND)

Doming (coarse-grinding) the Lake Superior agate   DIANE MAGNUSON

Doming (coarse-grinding) the Purple Passion agate   DIANE MAGNUSON

Domed Lake Superior agate after coarse-grinding

Domed Purple Passion agate after coarse-grinding   DIANE MAGNUSON

STEP 3: FINE-GRIND DOME

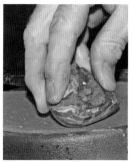

Fine-grinding the Lake Superior agate

Fine-grinding the Purple Passion agate
DIANE MAGNUSON

Domed Lake Superior agate after fine-grinding

Domed Purple Passion agate after fine-grinding   DIANE MAGNUSON

STEP 4: COARSE-SAND DOME

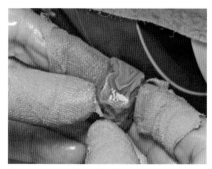

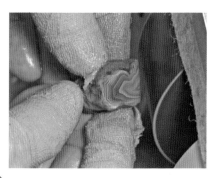

Coarse-sanding the Lake Superior agate

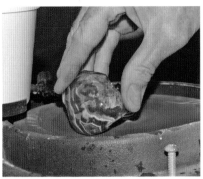

Coarse-sanding the Purple Passion agate   DIANE MAGNUSON

Domed Lake Superior agate after coarse-sanding

Domed Purple Passion agate after coarse-sanding   DIANE MAGNUSON

STEP 5: FINE-SAND DOME

Fine-sanding the Lake Superior agate

Fine-sanding the Purple Passion agate
DIANE MAGNUSON

STEP 5: FINE-SAND DOME (continued)

Domed Lake Superior agate after fine-sanding

Domed Purple Passion agate after fine-sanding   DIANE MAGNUSON

STEP 6: PREPOLISH

Prepolishing the Lake Superior agate

Prepolishing the Purple Passion agate
DIANE MAGNUSON

Domed Lake Superior agate after prepolishing

Domed Purple Passion agate after prepolishing   DIANE MAGNUSON

STEP 7: POLISH

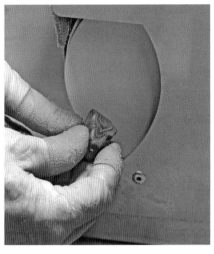

Polishing the Lake Superior agate

  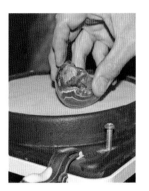

Polishing the Purple Passion agate   DIANE MAGNUSON

Fully polished, domed Lake Superior agate

Fully polished, domed Purple Passion agate   DIANE MAGNUSON

REPLACING YOUR DISCS AND WHEELS

When it begins to take you two to three times as long to complete a given stage as it did when the disc was new, that usually means it's time to replace one or more of your discs or wheels. With flat lap discs, you have two options: you can either buy complete discs with backer plates or you can just purchase new top plates and put them onto your original backer plates. While the process for removing and replacing top plates is somewhat involved, there's considerable cost savings: For a full set of five discs, it's $160 for top plates only and $410 for completely new discs. With cabber wheels, you simply need to buy a new wheel; some people try to refinish their wheels, but *it's not worth the cost or effort.*

PROCESS FOR REPLACING DISC TOP PLATES FOR FLAT LAPS AND SLANT LAPS:

1. Use heat gun to heat up the disc across the full surface to loosen the glue.

2. Use a putty knife to pry the top and backer plates apart (you might want to wear work gloves to avoid injury).

3. Optionally, use WD-40 to spray into the gap between the top plate and the backer plate to loosen the top plate.

4. After rubbing off excess glue and WD-40, use acetone to remove any remaining glue residue.

5. Peel away the pressure-sensitive adhesive (PSA) paper from your new top plate.

6. Carefully align the center hole of the new top plate with the hole on the backer plate, and then ease the top plate onto the backer plate.

7. Press firmly all the way around the top plate. Let sit for an hour before using.

CABOCHON MAKING AND FACE-POLISHING TIPS SUMMARY

- The ultra-coarse rough-grinding stage should be performed with care; otherwise, it's easy to create deep scratches in your gemstones that will be difficult to remove. Consider face-cutting stones that have too much excess material or deep surface flaws before you start your grinding operations.

- Inspecting stones carefully at the end of each processing stage is the "secret sauce" of polishing. Master this part of the process and you are well on your way to creating beautiful, high-gloss gems.

- Process your gemstones in batches and set them in a series of plastic trays to represent the next stage to be performed. This will dramatically improve your productivity and help your work be more consistent.

- With each processing stage, your excitement will mount. Avoid the temptation to rush ahead and make sure you are truly finished with that stage by inspecting your stones carefully.

- Take good care of your grinding, sanding, and polishing discs, and they will produce a large quantity of beautifully polished stones. Keep them upright in a dish rack and cover them with a small towel to protect them from dust, oil spray, and debris, all of which will reduce their effectiveness.

- To get a nicely contoured dome on your stones, follow the natural surface contours of the stone as much as possible as you sand it with rocking and sweeping motions accompanied by rotational movement. "Think in 3D" as you make these motions to envision the finished surface and feel how the stone is conforming to the desired shape and contour.

CHAPTER 6: DRILLING

OVERVIEW

Drilling gemstones is a lapidary operation used to create a hole through or into gemstone pendants. While it's not complicated, it requires considerable patience and use of fine motor skills. There are two ways to drill a stone. One is to lay your cabochon flat and then drill all the way through it; this is generally referred to as **face-drilling**. The other option, referred to as **top-drilling**, involves drilling partway into the top of a stone or cabochon to allow insertion of a jewelry post, which is then inserted into the drill hole and fastened with adhesive. Drilling gemstones is entirely different than working with ordinary home improvement and woodworking drills. Instead of applying constant pressure, when using a lapidary drill it's essential to use a **press-and-release** technique that is repeated numerous times.

LAPIDARY EQUIPMENT AND SUPPLIES NEEDED

Drilling stones requires a specialized lapidary drill press and diamond-coated drill bits. These machines allow for a high level of precision and have a high-torque, variable-speed motor. Machines with minimum speeds of less than 2,000 rpm are preferred for softer and more valuable gemstone materials, but these machines cost significantly more. You can also purchase a coolant system that sprays fluid onto the surface of the stone; this not only prevents your diamond drill bits from getting burned out too quickly but also reduces chipping and fracturing of the gemstone materials. For most beginning to intermediate hobbyists, it's simpler to just immerse the stones you're drilling in water as a means of keeping the drill bits and stones cool enough for drilling.

TIME REQUIREMENTS

Drilling is a relatively quick process, taking about 3–5 minutes per pendant stone. It might take more or less time depending on the thickness of the stone when face-drilling or the depth of the hole needed when top-drilling. The hardness of the gemstone material is also a factor. Softer stones like quartz take less time, while harder stones like agate take longer.

RECOMMENDED EQUIPMENT AND SUPPLIES

Dremel drill station
RICHARD PAUPORE

EuroTool 6-millimeter benchtop drill press

Micro-Mark MicroLux 3-speed mini drill press

Many people attempt to use hardware and home improvement–grade drills and bits to drill through gemstones, but these tools are only a recipe for broken and chipped stones and ruined drill bits. Also, while there are commercial drill presses that can be adapted to lapidary drilling processes, you'll be better served by a machine that has been purpose-built for lapidary work. These machines aren't more expensive; they just have lower rpm settings necessary for drilling hard gemstone materials.

We recommend the EuroTool benchtop drill press for both beginner and intermediate lapidary artists. As shown below, there are three pulleys underneath the

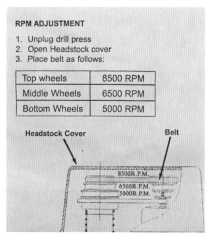

RPM ADJUSTMENT

1. Unplug drill press
2. Open Headstock cover
3. Place belt as follows:

Top wheels	8500 RPM
Middle Wheels	6500 RPM
Bottom Wheels	5000 RPM

Speed settings and belt and pulleys for EuroTool benchtop drill press top cover that allow you to adjust the speed by simply moving the orange cover belt onto one of the pulleys. The speed ranges for each pulley are as follows, and you can adjust the speed from low to high with the dial on the right side of the drill press:

- **Bottom pulley:** 810–4,800 rpm

- **Middle pulley:** 1,250–8,500 rpm

- **Top pulley:** 2,200–12,600 rpm

If you want to use a coolant system that sprays coolant onto the surface of the stones you're drilling (rather than immersing them in water), you can optionally purchase the Micro-Mark MicroFlow Coolant System or the flex cooler and pump system from Kingsley North.

DRILLING SUPPLIES

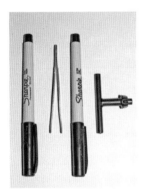

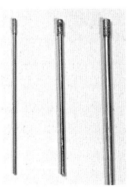

Tweezers, fine-point permanent markers, and drill chuck

For most drilling, it's best to purchase relatively inexpensive diamond-tipped, solid-core drill bits ranging from 1.5 millimeters to 2.5 millimeters.

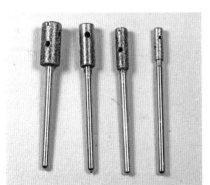

While hollow-core bits have a somewhat longer useful life, the increased cost is generally not worth the extended usage you get. That said, for bits ranging from 3 millimeters to 6 millimeters, it's best to purchase hollow-core bits.

A small tray to hold the cutting board and excess water or coolant. If you are immersing the cutting board and stone in water, the tray needs to be deep enough so that the stone is fully submerged. When drilling, we recommend doing so on a small piece of wood such as a 1-by-4-inch piece of pine. The board needs to fit snugly in your tray so that it doesn't float. A small sponge on top of your piece of wood helps when drilling domed or rounded cabochons from the back. It also helps when drilling uneven pieces like a small whole agate because it helps hold the stone steady. When drilling flat stones and cabochons, you won't need the sponge.

When you're top-drilling, it's helpful to have a small vise to hold gemstones steady.

HELPFUL TIP We recommend using 2-millimeter drill bits for the jewelry projects featured in this book that require face-drilled cabochons. Smaller holes can make it difficult to attach jump rings or pinch bails, and larger holes will be somewhat unsightly unless you are threading a cord through the drill hole without use of jump rings or clasps.

SETUP AND OPERATION

Lapidary drill presses are quiet and don't create much of a mess. They are also highly portable, so you can set them up in any well-lit area. It essential to have a bright desk lamp nearby to make inspecting your progress easier.

THREE TYPES OF DRILLING

FACE-DRILLING

Face-drilling means drilling all the way through a jewelry pendant or cabochon while it is lying flat. The stone is kept steady by holding it firmly with your thumb and first two fingers, or you can use soft clay or a small sponge on top of the cutting board to keep the stone more secure. We recommend against drilling through gemstone pieces thicker than 5–7 millimeters, especially when it comes to very hard stones, such as agate or jasper. For jewelry pieces, we recommend that you drill the stone partway through from each side to avoid chipping and breaking on the back side of the stone as the drill bit comes through.

TOP-DRILLING

Top-drilling means drilling a hole approximately 5–7 millimeters into the top of the gemstone material so that you can glue a jewelry post, such as an eyepin, into the top of the stone for attaching a chain or cord. During drilling, the stones are held steady by a miniature vise that sits atop a small hardwood block. If you will be doing a lot of top-drilling, you might even go as far as to permanently secure the mini vise to the wooden block to further reduce any movement while drilling. When top-drilling, you need to carefully inspect the stone to ensure there aren't existing fractures, which can cause breaks during the drilling process. You also need to ensure that the top of the stone is wide (thick) enough; generally speaking, the surface of the stone that you will be drilling into should be at least two times the diameter of the hole you're planning on drilling.

HELPFUL TIP The top-drilling method can also be used to make jewelry beads. You'll need to use 3- to 6-millimeter hollow-core drill bits to go through beads greater than 8 millimeters in length or diameter.

DRILLING A WHOLE STONE

One popular additional drilling application is drilling through whole stones, such as a small natural rough agate or a rounded stone bead, and placing on a necklace chain or cord either directly or after putting a jump ring onto the stone. While this seems straightforward, it requires additional patience, and we recommend using 3- to 6-millimeter hollow core drill bits to go through stones or beads greater than 4 millimeters in thickness or diameter. Depending on the thickness of the piece you are drilling through, you might need to periodically stop and tap out the gemstone material from inside the core of the drill bit.

CRITICAL DRILLING TIPS

DRILLING STONE VS. DRILLING WOOD

When it comes to drilling, using a lapidary drill is entirely different than working with ordinary woodworking drills or power tools. In a woodworking drill, the drill immediately "bites" into the surface of the wood, and you achieve the desired drilling depth by exerting consistent downward pressure (as opposed to the press-and-release technique described on page 126). Because drilling stones is entirely different, you should not attempt to use a lapidary drill in the same way you would use a woodworking drill.

WHEN TO REPLACE DRILL BITS

The drill bits we recommend will yield only three to five drilled stones, especially with harder materials like agate and jasper. It's time to replace the bit if you notice a small black stream coming off the tip of the bit, the diamond coating has worn off the tip, or you aren't making any further progress drilling into the stone. Pressing harder will only result in damaging the piece you are drilling.

DRILLING PROCESS STEP-BY-STEP

STEP 1: SET DRILL SPEED AS DESIRED

DRILLING METHODS COMPARED

STEP	FACE-DRILLING (LAPIS CABOCHON)	TOP-DRILLING (AGATE)	DRILLING WHOLE STONE (AGATE)
1. Mark stone with marker.			
2. Drill face side up using press-and-release technique.			
3. Flip stone and mark back side.		NA	
4. Drill from back.		NA	
5. Finished pieces			

Once you are ready to start drilling, set the drill press speed to the lowest possible setting that will produce results. Lower rpm settings will extend the life of your diamond-coated drill bits and make it less likely that you will damage the pieces you are drilling. However, with drill presses that have very low speed settings like 1,000 rpm, it can take quite a long time to complete your drill holes. For most of our usage and testing, we use a speed of 3,000-5,000 rpm with the belt on the middle pulley as shown previously; this seems to strike a nice balance between preserving drill bits, not damaging your gemstones, and getting the task done efficiently.

STEP 2: PLACE DRILL BIT

Place your drill bit so that it protrudes just far enough to go through the pieces you are drilling plus an additional 2–4 millimeters to keep the bottom tip of the drill chuck out of the water tray; otherwise, you'll get excessive wobble when making the initial impression on the stone.

STEP 3: MARK YOUR STONE WITH A FINE-POINT MARKER

You can mark both front and back either by using a double stencil or by using a pair of tweezers. If using tweezers, hold the stone with the tip of the tweezers just below the mark you made on the front of the stone, then flip the stone over and mark a corresponding point just above the tip of the tweezers on the back side. If your material is translucent, you can drill two-thirds to three-fourths of the way through the stone, then hold the stone up to light so that you can see the partial drill hole and mark the back side.

STEP 4: SET UP WATER TRAY

Fill your plastic (or steel) tray with water and place the small cutting board in the tray securely. It should have a tight fit so that it doesn't float. Add water so it covers the piece being drilled. Add or remove water while drilling.

STEP 5: IMMERSE STONE IN WATER

Hold securely with thumb and first two fingers. For additional stability, you can put soft clay or a sponge beneath the stone, as long as the stone's surface stays below water. The sponge is especially handy both when drilling the back side of a cabochon (because of the domed top surface) and when drilling rough natural stones that don't have flat surfaces.

STEP 6: BEGIN DRILLING

Press drill bit against stone, lightly at first and then with moderate pressure until you feel the bit gripping the stone and a stream of gemstone material flows out from the stone. The bit might dance or skitter around the smooth, wet surface, and your first instinct will be to press harder to try to get traction—this is the exact opposite of what you need to do! Instead of pushing even harder, let the drill bit do its work.

HELPFUL TIP If you are getting too much vibration, the drill bit is telling you to ease back and apply less pressure until you've begun to penetrate the stone's surface. It might also be telling you that your drill bit is extended too far out of the drill chuck or that the stone itself is not being held securely enough for drilling.

STEP 7: PRESS AND RELEASE

Once the drill has clearly begun to cut into the stone, you'll need to avoid another common instinct: driving the bit through the rest of the stone. Instead, press the bit down a little, then pull back, and then repeat this process. Apply moderate pressure and use only enough pressure to ensure the drill is actually doing some work, as evidenced by a small milky-white stream of material coming out of the drill hole. This ensures you aren't overheating the tip of the drill bit and allows the cooling lubricant to flush the drill hole and cool the bit. You'll actually learn the press-and-release technique rather quickly once you get going; if you're doing it incorrectly, you'll notice that your diamond drill bits are burning out.

The press-and-release movement is actually more akin to a pulsing motion with 1-second intervals: 1 second pressing the drill down into the stone, 1 second up. When you are first learning, you should count out loud, pressing down on the odd numbers and lifting up off the stone completely on the even ones. For hard gemstone materials like agate and jasper with 5–7 millimeter thickness, it can take 50–100 presses to get all the way through the stone. This is where patience is critical because pressing harder just burns the diamond coating off of the drill bit more quickly with little to no additional progress in creating the hole.

STEP 8: MONITOR YOUR PROGRESS
When Face-Drilling

As you get into a rhythm of drilling, continually monitor how far the drill bit is getting into the gemstone. For face-drilled stones, you want to gradually ease up on the pressure as you get farther into the stone. To assess progress, it's best to turn off the drill press and then visually inspect how deep the bit goes into the partial drill hole in relation to the thickness of the piece you are drilling. Easing up on pressure has two advantages: 1) If you're drilling all the way through a stone, it minimizes breakout on the reverse side of the stone. 2) If you're going to be flipping the stone over and drilling from the back side (which is what we generally recommend), easing up on pressure prevents you from accidentally drilling all the way through and allows for a consistent, smooth hole on each side of the stone.

HELPFUL TIP When in doubt, check your work. Always remember that when face-drilling, you can always stop drilling and hold your stone up to your desk lamp. If you can clearly see the drill hole from the back side, then dry off the stone, mark the spot on the back side, and resume drilling from back to front.

When Top-Drilling

Here you don't have to worry about breakout or chipping. Instead, your primary concern is drilling only as deep as necessary to set your jewelry post and adhesive. This results in a more secure setting for your post and ensures that the cooling lubricant is getting to the tip of the drill bit (it can't if the drill bit is too deep in the stone), which ultimately limits the wear on your drill bits.

DRILLING TIPS SUMMARY

- Allow the bit to extend out of the drill only as much as needed to achieve the depth of the hole that you'll be drilling and to keep the bottom tip of the drill chuck out of the water tray. This reduces wobble and thus slows heat buildup.

- For stones that aren't flat, you'll need to secure them with something like soft molding clay or a sponge. Another great option is plumber's putty. Do not use Play-Doh!

- Choosing which side to drill into: If only one surface will be showing in your jewelry piece, start by drilling into the side that will show. If both surfaces will be displayed, it's best to drill from both sides rather than drilling all the way through from one side; this eliminates the "breakout" effect.

- Drill at a slow to moderate speed, as it keeps the heat to a minimum, thus reducing premature wear of the diamond abrasives on the tip of the drill bit. However, with drill presses that have very low speed settings like 1,000 rpm, it can take quite a long time to complete your drill holes. For most of our usage and testing, we use a 3,000–5,000 rpm speed, which strikes a nice balance between preserving drill bits, not damaging your gemstones, and getting the drilling task done efficiently.

DRILLING

CHAPTER 7:
ROTARY HAND TOOL
APPLICATIONS

OVERVIEW

Rotary hand tools, such as Dremels, can be used to make an extensive variety of lapidary artworks and jewelry pieces, such as carvings and engravings. They can also be used for polishing gemstones, especially those that are softer, like Petoskey stones. And while there is no substitute for lapidary saws, drills, or flat lapidary grinding-and-polishing machines, Dremels can perform many of the same operations, just on a smaller scale. Additionally, they can work in tandem with these other machines by performing tasks for which those machines are not well suited, such as creating concave contours and shapes that flat laps can't or widening, smoothing out, and polishing drill holes made by lapidary drill presses.

Because there is such a wide range of applications for hand tools, there's no set process that encompasses all project types and activities. With each application, you'll start by determining whether you want to work strictly with the Dremel tool or with a **flex-shaft attachment.** Then you'll select the bits, accessories, and supplies needed to complete your project. There can easily be 10 pieces needed, including the tools to swap out different bits or attachments, so it's important to have them laid out before you get started.

And many rotary tool activities are performed in conjunction with other operations, such as cutting (sawing) and cabochon making. Most also involve a lot of personal creativity, enabling you to quickly learn and adapt your skills to the things you enjoy most. For the sample projects included in this chapter, we will list the materials needed, the time requirements, and any supplemental operations involved.

One note about materials is that softer materials are great for beginners because they're easier to work with. For example, basalt (which is not a gemstone) can be a great stone for creating shapes and carvings because it's soft, presents nicely, and can usually be obtained at no cost just by harvesting some local river rock or beach rock (where permitted).

LAPIDARY EQUIPMENT AND SUPPLIES NEEDED

The simplest setup involves a rotary hand tool such as the Dremel 3000. If you plan to do more-intricate work, such as stone carving, you'll probably want to get a flex-shaft attachment with a corresponding hand tool and a foot pedal either to toggle the tool on and off or, if you have a more advanced tool such as the Foredom K.2230, to vary the speed. There's an extensive variety of bits to choose from, and many of them come in sets selected for the kinds of tasks or pieces you intend to create. Most of the bits use crushed diamonds for drilling, cutting, shaping, and sanding. Finally, there are other tools and supplies to consider, like a hanger for the flex-shaft attachment, a benchtop vise, and a water-drip system.

GEMSTONE MATERIALS

Rotary hand tools can be used with any of the gemstones listed in the table on pages 18–19, and it can work with many more. Among the sample projects we've included are a basalt stone and a Petoskey stone because they are both softer than other stones like agates and jaspers, and hence easier to work with, especially for beginning hobbyists.

TIME REQUIREMENTS

Perhaps the best thing about working with rotary tools (in addition to the flexibility and creativity) is the small amount of time required to perform different tasks and complete different types of artworks. Of course, there are no limitations to your creativity, and as you develop your skills, you'll begin to create more-intricate designs and pieces, such as detailed art carvings that incorporate and enhance the natural beauty of the gemstones you are working with. As with all other lapidary skills in this book, we recommend that you start with simple projects and build your confidence along with your skills.

RECOMMENDED EQUIPMENT AND SUPPLIES

EQUIPMENT

While there are numerous makers of rotary hand tools, they are often referred to by hobbyists as "Dremels." One other terminology point that's worth mentioning is the use of the word *bit,* which can signify a disc for grinding, sanding, and polishing; a bit for drilling; or a bit for cutting and carving.

Rotary hand tools are a super-affordable way to get started in the lapidary arts hobby. As with other types of lapidary equipment, it's important to choose tools that have stood the test of time in terms of quality, features, and reliability. And because there are so many makers, we've narrowed our recommendations to the top standard rotary tool (Dremel) and top flex-shaft tool (Foredom).

Flex-shaft attachments can be purchased for the Dremel, but they are limited in that they don't provide variable-speed-control capability. We tried out one of the considerably less expensive tools and quickly discovered issues with its sturdiness and reliability. As with other types of lapidary equipment, working with lower-priced and lower-quality brands will frequently lead to frustration and poor results.

At the top of the list for standard rotary tools is the Dremel 3000, and it's there for a reason. It's the number one proven tool used by countless lapidary artists. Additionally, it comes with many of the bits and attachments needed by both beginner and experienced hobbyists. Note that in the table below we've included a flex-shaft tool attachment and hanger for Dremel. The Dremel tool itself is $75. The flex-shaft attachment is $35. The hanger is $17 and is critical to keep the flex shaft straight and avoid damaging or breaking the shaft. The foot pedal (not made by Dremel) is $19; it provides a convenient on–off toggle for rotary hand tools when using a flex-shaft attachment but does not provide variable speed control.

The Foredom K.2230 is our top recommendation for a pure flex-shaft tool with its own variable-speed motor (i.e., it's not an attachment but a tool itself); it has well-proven performance and durability and has gained wide acceptance with hobbyists who do fine-detailed lapidary work. It comes with a foot pedal.

MAKE AND MODEL	COST	MAX SPEED (RPM)	MIN SPEED (RPM)	VOLTS	FLEX SHAFT	FOOT PEDAL**
Dremel 3000-1/24*	$146 (includes flex shaft, pedal, and hanger	35,000	5,000	120	Optional	Optional
Foredom K.2230	$423 (includes hanger)	18,000	0	115	Included	Included
Dremel 4000-4/34*	$167 (includes flex shaft, pedal and hanger)	35,000	5,000	120	Optional	Optional

* For Dremel tools, the first number after the model number is the number of attachments, and the second is the number of accessories (e.g., *1/24* means one attachment and 24 accessories).

** Dremel-compatible (the price listed above is for the Temo brand)

SUPPLIES

When it comes to supplies, there's a daunting list of bit sets and other add-ons that can expand or enhance the performance and processes for rotary hand tools. The Dremel comes with a nice starter set of bits and attachments, so take some time to inspect what's included and to work with the items that come with your tool before purchasing additional items. The items and examples we've curated below are well suited for the most common lapidary applications, including those we use for illustration in this book. Additionally, you can download two handy reference posters from the Dremel website that will help orient you to the broader array of bits and accessories: the Dremel Rotary Accessory Guide (tinyurl.com/dremel-accessory-guide) and the Dremel Rotary Tool & Attachment Compatibility Chart (tinyurl.com/dremel-compatibility-chart).

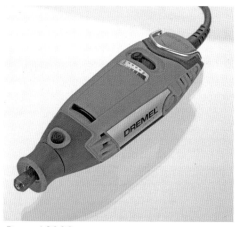

Dremel 3000   RICHARD PAUPORE

Dremel with drill press station   RICHARD PAUPORE

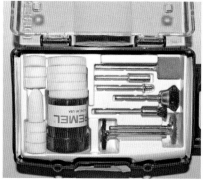

(Above left) Standard bit and accessory kit (included with Dremel 3000) for miscellaneous applications; (above right) Dremel 726-01 cleaning and polishing accessory kit ($15) for cleaning, polishing, and buffing

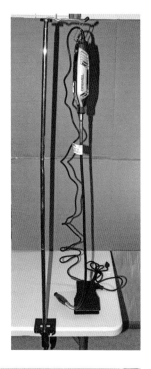

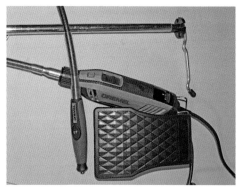

(Left and above) Dremel flex-shaft system with foot pedal and hanger

Foredom K.2230 flex-shaft tool

Oudtinx Dremel-compatible diamond bit set ($20) for stone-carving and engraving

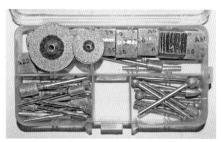

(Above left) Rocaris 40-pack 1-inch abrasive wheel wheel set ($10) for buffing and polishing; (above right) Drilax 50-piece diamond bit set ($25) for drilling, grinding, shaping, carving, and engraving

SUPPLIES *(continued)*

Submersible pump RICHARD PAUPORE

Flex cooler RICHARD PAUPORE

Zam buffing and polishing compound
($10 for 4 ounces)

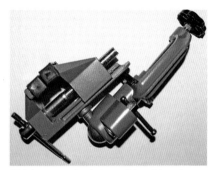

Tabletop swivel vise with rubber jaws
($20) to hold either a flex-shaft tool
or a stone so that you don't have to
hold both by hand

In addition to the items pictured on above and on pages 132–133, you will need:

- **Handheld lighted magnifier** (such as Carson; $10) or desk-mounted lighted magnifier to inspect your work in progress (pictured on page 86)

- **Small plastic tub** with sponge and wood board for both dipping and drilling (pictured on page 120). This can be used in place of the pump and flex-cooler system.

- **Safety goggles and face mask**

SAFETY

There are several important safety considerations when using hand tools:

- Turn the tool off and unplug it when changing bits.

- When working with metal-bonded grinding, cutting, and drilling bits, we recommend putting your pieces or the tool in a vise so that you aren't holding both the tool and the piece you're working on at the same time.

- Use water in a small plastic tub or from a drip system like the flex cooler to capture fine dust particles.

- Use an N95 or KN95 mask or a respirator and wear safety goggles when cutting, grinding, or drilling. This is especially important when you're working with toxic gemstone materials like malachite.

- Work in a well-ventilated area.

GETTING STARTED WORKING WITH HAND TOOLS

There are many videos that provide you with a quick start to using the Dremel tool, common types of bits and their uses, and how to go about changing bits. Rather than summarizing this basic operational information in this book, we suggest watching one of the videos such as the Dremel Beginners Video (youtube .com/watch?v=D_tazz0uHqk), and we will instead put our focus on step-by-step processes for some of the most common rotary hand tool applications for lapidary work.

Because of the variability in applications for rotary hand tools, there's not a consistent path for developing your skills and confidence. That said, here are a few suggestions and starting points that will serve you well when you're just beginning.

- Start with cheaper and softer stones like basalt to get comfortable working with the tools.

- Consider using a benchtop vise to hold your pieces securely, especially for carving. For flex-shaft applications, you might place your tool in the vise and move the stone you're working with against the bits on the tool.

- Start with projects that can be completed with just the rotary hand tool. Once you're comfortable with that, you can begin to use the flex shaft and its related attachments, including the hanger and foot pedal.

SAMPLE PROJECTS

The sample projects we've chosen can be completed by beginner to intermediate hobbyists. Some are complete projects using only the given rotary hand tool(s) and attachments, and some are supplemental to other lapidary applications, such as drilling a cabochon that was made by sawing and grinding. There's a mix of projects that use either the rotary hand tool by itself or with the flex shaft.

PROJECT 1: DRILLING A CARVED BASALT PENDANT

What will be made: A hole will be drilled into a carved basalt pendant so it can be put onto a chain or cord and worn as a necklace.

Difficulty: Low

Time requirement: 10 minutes

Materials used: Carved basalt pendant

Tools and supplies needed: Rotary hand tool with flex shaft, hanger, and pedal (see page 133); water pump and flexible drip system; solid-core 2-millimeter drill bit and wide and narrow cone drill bits

Solid-core drill bit and cone drill bits

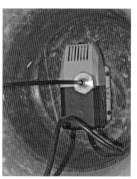

Water pump and flexible drip system

Setup

1. Set up the pump and flexible water-drip system (or a small tub of water).

2. Use a fine-point permanent marker to mark where the hole will be drilled.

3. Attach the 2-millimeter drill bit to the rotary hand tool.

4. Set the tool to speed level 3.

Step 1: Initial Drilling

Turn on the rotary hand tool and apply light to moderate pressure at the point you marked. Use a rotational motion, tilting the drill bit slightly while drilling farther into the stone until the hole is complete.

Step 2: Widen and Smooth Out Drill Hole

Using the wide cone bit, widen and smooth out the hole from both the front and the back of the piece. Once again, use a rotational motion, applying pressure evenly around the perimeter of the initial hole.

Step 3: Widen Inner Perimeter of Drill Hole

Using the narrow cone bit, widen the inner perimeter of the hole.

Tips for Success

- Use lighter pressure as you get close to completing the drill hole to reduce the chance for large breaks and chipping.

- Marking the drilling spot on the back side and drilling from both sides helps to reduce larger chips and breaks.

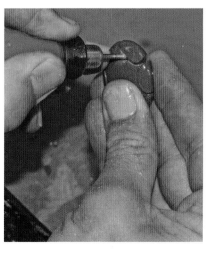

PROJECT 2: BASALT SMILEY FACE CARVING

What will be made: Carved basalt stone with a smiley face for display and decoration that can also be made into a pendant

Difficulty: Low

Time requirement: 10 minutes

Materials used: Small lake-tumbled basalt stone

Tools and supplies needed: Rotary hand tool with flex shaft, hanger, and pedal (see page 133); water pump and flexible drip system (see page 134); nailhead cutting bit, large and small inverted-cone bits, and fine sanding disc bit

Setup

1. Set up the pump and flexible water-drip system (or use a small tub of water).

2. Attach the large inverted-cone bit to the rotary hand tool.

3. Set the tool to speed level 3 or 4.

Step 1: Draw the Face with a Fine-Point Marker

Step 2: Carve the outer eye rings.

After attaching the large inverted-cone bit, gradually rotate the edge of the bit into the outer circle of one eye, and then work around the full circle, with the bit nearly parallel to the surface. Repeat for the second eye.

Step 3: Carve the smile.

After attaching the nailhead cutting bit, ease the edge of the bit into one corner of the mouth, and then gradually work across to the other side.

Step 4: Carve the pupils.

After attaching the small inverted-cone bit, gradually rotate the edge of the bit into the inner circle of one eye, and then work around the full circle, with the bit nearly parallel to the surface. Repeat for the second eye.

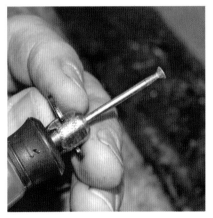 

Step 5: Remove scratches and give a semigloss glow.

After attaching the fine sanding disc, work the full face with rotational movement, making sure to cover the outer edges.

PROJECT 3: PETOSKEY STONE (FOSSIL) FACE-POLISHING

Note that you will start with a coarse sanding disc rather than a grinding disc because Petoskey stones are soft limestone–based fossils. Also, the stone we're using already has a smooth, lake-tumbled finish.

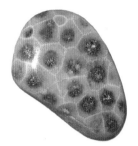

What will be made: Face-polished Petoskey stone

Difficulty: Low   **Time requirement:** 10 minutes

Materials used: Petoskey stone found on a lakeshore (below left)

Tools and supplies needed: Rotary hand tool, water tub (or water pump and flexible drip system), sanding and polishing disc bits, polishing compound

Setup

1. Set up the small water tub to immerse or periodically dip the pendant into (or set up the pump and flexible drip system).

2. Use a fine-point permanent marker to mark where the drill hole will be made.

3. Attach the rough sanding disc bit to the rotary hand tool.

4. Set the tool to speed level 3.

Step 1: Coarse-Sand

Sand the full face and edges of the stone, periodically dipping in water to minimize airborne rock dust and scratching of the stone.

Step 2: Fine-Sand

Fine-sand the full face and edges of the stone, periodically dipping in water.

Step 3: Prepolish

Prepolish the full face and edges of the stone, periodically dipping in water. Note the semigloss finish after this step.

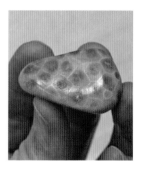

Step 2

Step 3

Step 4: Polish

Apply polishing compound to the buffing-and-polishing bit and polish the full face of the stone. Note that we had to switch the collets that hold the polishing bits because of their wider shafts.

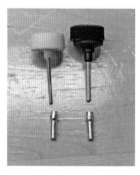

PROJECT 4: MOON CONCAVE-SURFACE SHAPING

This is one major step of a larger process that involves the use of a lapidary saw and flat lapidary grinding-and-polishing machine. The rotary hand tool is used to create concave shape contours that can't be created on the flat lap machine. The pieces will be finished on the flat lap (see page 151).

What will be made: Shaping of the inner curve of a moon-shaped cabochon

Difficulty: Low

Time requirement: 5–10 minutes

Materials used: Shaped cabochon with unfinished inner curve

Tools and supplies needed: Rotary tool, grinding disc, saw dressing stick, water tub (or pump and flexible drip system)

Setup
1. Insert the grinding disc into rotary hand tool.

2. Set up the water tub.

Step 1: Grind the Inner Surface to Shape
Gradually work the grinding disc around the inner contour, periodically dipping the piece in water.

Step 2: Clean Off Excess Gemstone Material
Use a saw blade dressing stick to periodically remove excess material.

Step 3: Repeat the Grinding Process to Smooth Rough Spots
Work the piece with continuous motion to get a smooth inner contour.

Step 1   Step 2   Step 3

Step 4: Sand and Polish the Inner Contour (Optional)
This step can be done to produce a more highly polished inner contour.

PROJECT 5: COMPLEX LABRADORITE CARVING

What will be made: Labradorite owl carving with drill hole that can be worn as a necklace pendant

Difficulty: Medium–high

Time requirement: 30-45 minutes

Materials used: Oval labradorite cabochon

Tools and supplies needed: Cabber machine; Dremel tool with flex-shaft attachment, hanger, and foot pedal (see page 133); water pump and flexible drip system (see page 134); nail-head cutting bit, 2-millimeter drill bit, and large and small inverted-cone bits (pictured on page 136)

Setup

1. Set up pump and flexible water-drip system (or a small tub of water to immerse or periodically dip the pendant into).

2. Attach the 2 millimeter drill bit to Dremel tool.

3. Set the tool to speed level 3 or 4.

Step 1: Draw the Owl Design with a Marker

Use both freehand drawing and a stencil for geometric shapes like the eyes and the beak.

Step 2: Create a Drill Hole to Attach a Necklace Cord

Follow all the steps in Project 1 (page 136) for creating an initial drill hole and then widening and smoothing with cone bits. Using the cone bit also allows you to clean up any chips or other imperfections and creates a smoother inner perimeter that won't cut a cloth or leather cord.

Step 3: Carve the Outer Eye Rings And Pupils

Follow Steps 2 and 4 in Project 2 (page 138).

Step 4: Carve the Remaining Owl Features

After attaching the small nailhead cutting bit, ease the edge of the bit into each remaining feature of the design, then gradually work along the sketched lines.

Step 5: Use a Cabber Machine to Sand and Polish the Piece

Start with the coarse sanding wheel, then the fine sanding and prepolish wheels; make sure to cover the outer edges.

148

CHAPTER 8:
JEWELRY MAKING

AN INTRODUCTION TO STYLES AND TECHNIQUES

There are likely as many jewelry styles as there are types of gemstones. But we would like to provide a brief introduction to a few jewelry-making styles and techniques that can be readily learned by beginners and that utilize the lapidary skills covered in this book. We won't cover things like silversmithing or wire wrapping since those require intensive training to produce consistent and good-quality results.

To make the different types of jewelry shown in this chapter you'll need an assortment of jewelry fittings like jump rings, glue-on bails, pinch bails (aka pinch clasps), and earring hooks. These fittings are commonly referred to as jewelry findings. There's an endless array of findings, just as there are countless jewelry styles. You can get most of the findings we show on either Etsy or Amazon or in craft stores and lapidary supply businesses,. They're quite inexpensive unless you decide that you want 925 silver (sterling silver) or gold findings. Start small and simple by choosing a couple of the jewelry projects in this chapter and acquiring the findings needed for those projects.

Remember to keep your gemstone materials in focus as you develop your own creations. And, as many lapidary artists say, "Let the stone lead you." For additional inspiration, there are numerous websites that offer jewelry equipment, supplies, and tutorials. You can also find help by visiting local craft stores or joining a rock club; many offer classes to get you started.

SUPPLIES

Pendant pinch bails

Pendant pinch bails

Glue-on bails

Earring hooks with
pinch clasps

Post earring base

Eyepin

Jump rings

Pliers and clippers

Jewelry adhesive, toothpicks, razor
blade, fine sandpaper, tray for gluing

Magnifying eyeglasses (cheaters)

150

SAMPLE PROJECTS

PROJECT 1: NECKLACE PENDANTS, EARRINGS, AND BRACELET CHARMS WITH FACE-DRILLED CABOCHONS AND JUMP RINGS

A gemstone that has been face-drilled (drilled through from front to back) is easy to attach to a chain or cord with the use of a jump ring or pinch bail. This project requires a finished gemstone that has been face-drilled, as described in the Chapter 6 (page 121). As noted in that chapter, we generally recommend a 2-millimeter drill hole to accommodate jump rings and pinch bails. Also note that the drill hole needs to be positioned close enough to the top of the cabochon that jump rings and bails can be attached.

Several types of jewelry can be made with cabochons that have been face-drilled. The most common examples are pictured below. All the jewelry types in this project are extremely simple to make. The process steps are the same for each type of jewelry shown.

Face-drilled lapis pendant with jump ring and chain

Face-drilled tiger's-eye pendant with pinch bail and chain

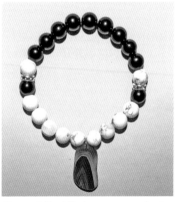

Face-drilled Botswana pendant
with jump ring and gemstone
bead bracelet

Earrings with earring hooks and jump rings

Tools and Supplies Needed

- Needle-nose or flat-nose pliers

- **Jump rings** of varying diameters (3 mm–10 mm)

- **Pinch bails**

- **Necklace chain or cord**

- **Earring hooks with bottom loops** that can be opened and closed

- **Earring hooks with pinch bails**

Step 1: Attach Jump Ring to Face-Drilled Cabochon

Note: Jump rings are small pieces of wire that have been formed into a circle (you can make your own using the same type of wire that's used for wire wrapping), so when we refer to the "ends" of a jump ring we are referring to the ends of the original piece of wire.

1. Select a jump ring that's large enough to leave space between it and the top of the cabochon to thread a chain or cord through; this is something of an art, but you'll get the hang of it pretty quickly.

2. Hold the jump ring with one hand and use the pliers in a twisting motion to open it so that the ends are offset, rather than pulling the ends directly apart from each other. This is critical to ensure the jump ring closes properly and retains its circular shape.

3. Insert one end of the jump ring through the drill hole on the top face until it protrudes out of the back. We like to start from the front because there's less

chance of scratching the face of the cabochon. If the jump ring or drill hole isn't big enough, you'll need a larger jump ring.

4. Use the pliers to close the jump ring from the back side until both ends of the ring are fully touching; this is important because a fine chain or beading thread can slip through very small openings. You might need to slightly bend the back-side end of the jump ring up and over the lip of your cabochon to get it aligned with the

A jump ring that has been opened as described in Step 1, No. 2

drill hole. If you are using the piece as a bracelet charm, you'll need to first place the charm with the open jump ring onto the bracelet and then close the jump ring.

5. Thread your necklace chain or cord through the jump ring. If there's not enough space for the chain or cord to slide freely, you'll need to remove the jump ring and use a larger one.

6. For earring hooks only: Use the pliers to open the loop at the bottom of the earring hook just as you open jump rings. Put the cabochon with jump ring onto the loop, then close the loop securely.

Step 2: Attach Pinch Bail to Face-Drilled Cabochon

This applies to both necklace pendants and earring hooks with pinch bails.

1. Select a pinch bail large enough to fit over the top of the cabochon from the front of the drill hole to the back.

2. Use pliers to open the bail wide enough to fit over the cabochon.

3. Insert one prong through the drill hole from the front of the cabochon, and then align the other prong with the drill hole on the back. We like to start from the front because there's less chance of scratching the face of the cabochon.

4. Pinch the clasp shut so that the prongs come together inside the drill hole.

5. For necklaces only: Thread your chain or cord through the attachment on the top of the bail.

PROJECT 2: NECKLACE PENDANTS AND CHARMS WITH GLUE-ON BAILS

Creating jewelry pieces using glue-on bails is one of the simplest of all jewelry-making methods, and it produces beautiful results. One of the main benefits of this method is that the front of your cabochon isn't covered by any hardware, such as a jump ring or clasp. A metal (such as silver-plated) bail is glued onto the flat back side of the cabochon, and then a chain or cord is threaded through a loop at the top of the bail.

Crazy lace agate heart pendant with glue-on bail and chain (finished piece shown on page 148)

Fairburn agate pendant with glue-on bail and gemstone bead bracelet

Tools and Supplies Needed

- **Jewelry adhesive** that is durable, flexible, and waterproof, such as E6000. Alternatively, you can use a two-part epoxy for a somewhat stronger bond, but adhesives like E6000 are the standard.

- **Glue-on bails** that are small but sufficient to hold the cabochons used for jewelry making. The smaller the stone, the smaller the bail you want. Also, the bails must have an enclosed loop at the top through which to thread your chain or cord.

- **Toothpicks** for applying the adhesive

- **Small plastic tray** in which to put the adhesive

- **Razor blade or X-acto knife** to remove excess adhesive

- **Jewelry chains and cords** for necklaces, such as silver-plated chains or black waxed cords

Step-by-Step Instructions

1. Thoroughly clean and dry the back side of your cabochon using a degreasing dishwashing liquid.

2. Align the stone with the glue-on bail to determine how you'll be orienting the stone with the bail.

3. Squeeze a small amount of E6000 adhesive into your plastic tray.

4. Use a toothpick to pick up a small amount of adhesive and apply it to the bail. Use just enough to hold the stone and not so much that a large amount oozes out onto the stone.

5. Place the cabochon onto the bail and apply enough pressure to spread the adhesive.

6. Align the stone with the stem of the bail so that it's symmetrical and straight.

7. Allow at least 12 hours for the adhesive to fully cure (even if the instructions say it can cure more quickly).

8. Use a razor blade or X-acto knife to remove any excess adhesive, being careful not to apply pressure to the sides of the bail, which might loosen it from the cabochon.

9. Attach your chain or cord.

PROJECT 3: PREMADE BEZEL SETTINGS FOR NECKLACE PENDANTS, BRACELET CHARMS, AND RINGS

There is a wide variety of preformed bezel settings for gemstones. Some are quite simple, and others are ornate. They can be made from a wide range of materials, including stainless steel, silver-plated brass or bronze, 925 silver (sterling silver), or gold. The easiest bezel settings to work with have closed backs, or

Binghamite necklace pendant with silver bezel

Gemstone bracelet with bezel charm

trays, that make it easier to attach them with jewelers' adhesives. Other settings have open backs, so there's only a thin rim, or ledge, around the perimeter of the setting on which to apply adhesive and attach your cabochon. It's best to start with closed-back bezels.

Fairburn agate cabochon in men's adjustable silver ring base

Lake Superior agate cabochon with women's adjustable silver ring base

It's also best to start with settings that have standard sizes such as 13 by 18 millimeters or 18 by 25 millimeters (where the shorter dimension is the width). You want to make your cabochons using a stencil that conforms to these dimensions. Once you have your cabochon close to the stencil shape, you need to repeatedly test the fit and curvature to ensure it's snug, without noticeable gaps between the stone and the outer rim of the bezel setting. This is the most difficult aspect of creating jewelry pieces with premade bezel settings. Also, you cannot finish your cabochons in a tumbler since the tumbling process may remove too much material, leaving a gap between the cabochon and the bezel rim.

Tools and Supplies Needed

- **Bezel settings** that match the size of your cabochons (For necklace pendants, they must have an attached bail or loop to allow them to be hung on a necklace chain. This isn't necessary for ring settings or earring settings where the bezel is already attached to an earring hook or post.)

- **Fine-mesh sandpaper**

- **E6000 or equivalent waterproof adhesive** for metal and stone

- **Small plastic tray** in which to put the adhesive

- **Toothpicks** for applying adhesive

- **Chain or other necklace,** such as a black waxed cord

Step-by-Step Instructions

1. Thoroughly clean and dry the backside of your cabochon using a degreasing dishwashing liquid.

2. Use a tiny piece of sandpaper to make scratch marks on the inside of the bezel setting (this is for closed-back settings only), being careful not to scratch the outside of the setting. This process is sometimes referred to as key scratching. This process ensures a tighter bond between the stone and the setting.

3. Squeeze a small amount of adhesive into your plastic tray.

4. Use a toothpick to pick up a small amount of adhesive and apply it to the bezel setting, spreading it around evenly (so it's not in one concentrated blob). For open-back settings (such as the rings shown on the opposite page), use the toothpick to draw out "threads" of adhesive along the inner rim of the setting. (This process will take some time to master, so be patient and be willing to stop, wipe off all the adhesive, and try again. It's advisable to practice creating the adhesive threads in your plastic tray.)

5. Place the cabochon into the bezel setting and apply enough pressure so that the adhesive spreads out and adheres to the stone.

6. Allow at least 12 hours for the adhesive to fully cure (even if the instructions say it can cure more quickly).

PROJECT 4: TOP-DRILLED STONE WITH EYEPIN

A cabochon or gemstone (rough or polished) that has been top-drilled (drilled partway into the top of the stone) and then fitted with an eyepin makes for a clean and simple presentation. Eyepins are available in a wide variety of designs and colors, and they should be threaded for a stronger grip on the stone.

Top-drilled whole stone with eyepin and chain

Tools and Supplies Needed

- **A finished gemstone** that has been top-drilled as described in Chapter 6 (page 121). The drill hole should be approximately 2 millimeters wide and 5–7 millimeters deep; the depth should match the length of the post on the eyepin.

- **Eyepin** that fits the drill hole with room to apply adhesive

- **Jewelry adhesive**

- **Small plastic tray** in which to put the adhesive

- **Jump rings**

- **Necklace chain or cord,** or earring hooks with bottom loops that can be opened and closed

Step-by-Step Instructions

1. Put a small amount of jewelers' adhesive into a plastic tray.

2. Apply some adhesive to the eyepin, enough to hold it in place and fill the drill hole.

3. Set the piece in a place where it can stand upright for at least 12 hours for the adhesive to cure.

4. Gently remove excess adhesive with a razor blade or X-acto knife.

5. If your eye post loop is too small to thread your necklace chain or cord through, then open and attach a jump ring in the manner described in Jewelry Project 3 (page 155).

6. Thread your chain or cord through the jump ring.

7. For earrings: Open the bottom loop of the earring hook and attach the jump ring, then close the loop.

PROJECT 5: BEADS AND WHOLE STONES FOR NECKLACES AND BRACELETS

Stones and beads with a drill hole drilled from side to side, near the top of the stone, will be strung onto a small chain, cord, or string. All of the jewelry types in this project are extremely simple to make. To avoid repetition for necklace pendants, earrings, and bracelet charms, we'll simply describe the common processes that are the same for each type of jewelry shown.

Tools and Supplies Needed

- **Needle-nose pliers**
- **Large jump rings** of varying diameters (8–12 millimeters)
- **Necklace chain or cord**

Step-by-Step Instructions

Type 1: Natural agate drilled side to side with cord or chain. Thread your chain or cord through the drill hole. If you have a cord with an extender chain, you might need to first remove the jump ring, then thread the cord through the hole, reattach the extender chain, and close the jump ring.

Type 2: Natural agate drilled front to back with cord. Fold the cord at the center point and thread it through the front of the hole, then bring the other end of the cord (with the clasp) through the cord loop and tighten.

Type 3: Natural drilled agate with jump ring and cord. Follow the steps in Jewelry Project 1 (page 151) for jump rings and necklace chains or cords.

PROJECT 6: POST EARRINGS

Small cabochons will be glued onto blank earring posts. Making post earrings is similar to making jewelry with premade bezel settings, but it's considerably simpler because you don't need cabochons that fit exactly in your settings.

Tools and Supplies Needed

- **Post-earring blanks and backers**

- **Fine-mesh sandpaper**

- **E6000 or equivalent waterproof adhesive** for metal and stone

- **Small plastic tray** in which to put adhesive

- **Toothpicks** for applying adhesive

Step-by-Step Instructions

1. Thoroughly clean and dry the back side of your cabochons using a degreasing dishwashing liquid.

2. Use a tiny piece of sandpaper to make scratch marks on the earring blanks (this process is sometimes referred to as key scratching). This ensures a tighter bond between the stone and the setting.

3. Squeeze a small amount of E6000 adhesive into your plastic tray.

4. Use a toothpick to pick up a small amount of adhesive and apply it to the earring blank.

5. Place the cabochon face down and press the earring blank onto the back side of the cabochon; apply enough pressure so that the adhesive spreads out and adheres to the stone.

6. Allow at least 12 hours for the adhesive to fully cure (even if the instructions say it can cure more quickly).

GLOSSARY

Abrasive (or grit) A silicon carbide–based compound that is very hard and is used during tumbling to smooth out rough edges and prepare the surfaces of gemstones for polishing. Successively finer grit meshes are used as you progress through the tumbling stages.

Bail Any type of jewelry finding that's used to attach a cabochon to a necklace chain or earring hook. Examples include jump rings and glue-on bails.

Banding Alternating color bands characteristic of some gemstones (primarily agates). The best banding features have striking contrasts from one color to the next.

Bezel A grooved ring or metal cup made to encase a finished gemstone. The cup style has a closed back.

Burr 1) A protruding section of gemstone material left after cutting your stones in half or into slabs. No cut is ever perfect, but some leave a more noticeable burr to be cut or ground away. 2) A rotary drill bit made of carbide and used for cutting, shaping, or grinding.

Cabochon (or cab) A piece of gemstone material that has been cut and ground into a pleasing and symmetrical shape, usually for jewelry making. It might be a standard shape, such as an oval or rectangle, or it might be free-form.

Chamfer A beveled edge that is ground around the perimeter of a piece of gemstone material for the purpose of creating a sloped or domed surface. After creating a chamfer, subsequent grinding eventually removes the flat beveled edge and brings the surface of the gemstone to a smoothly contoured dome.

Cut slab A thinly cut (about ¼"–⅜" thick) slice of gemstone material.

Diamond polishing paste Finely ground diamond mixed into a paste that is spread onto face-polishing discs. The diamond paste performs the polishing of gemstones to a high-gloss shine.

Dome-polishing Grinding, shaping, and polishing one portion of a stone's surface to highlight its most beautiful features.

Doming The process of creating a beveled edge, or chamfer, on a rough or flat surface and then gradually removing surface material through a series of rocking and rotating motions using grinding and sanding discs coated with diamond abrasives.

Dremel Brand name for the most popular of rotary hand tools; often used synonymously with "rotary hand tool."

Dressing stick A bar of aluminum oxide used to expose additional crushed diamonds on sintered-rim saw blades as the blade cuts thin slices off the end of the bar.

Eyepin (or headpin) A small metal jewelry post that is glued into the top of a gemstone or bead; a necklace or bracelet chain can be threaded through a circular eye at the top of the stone.

Face The surface of a stone that will be cut and/or polished. It is generally the most attractive surface, exhibiting the most color and pattern.

Face-drilling Drilling a cabochon or slab all the way through from front to back.

Faceting Flat spots on a domed stone. These spots are visually unappealing and can result from pressing the stone or cabochon against the grinding disk and holding it in one place without rocking or rotating.

Face-polishing Grinding, shaping, and polishing the face (surface) of a whole stone that exhibits the most striking color and pattern and leaving the rest in its rough state.

Finding See *jewelry finding*.

Flat lapidary grinder-polisher (flat lap) A machine used for grinding, sanding, and polishing gemstone pieces using horizontal discs that spin at high speeds.

Grit See *abrasive*.

Headpin See *eyepin*.

High-gloss finish Otherwise known as a high polish, this is the final result of tumble-polishing and face-polishing. It can be obtained only through the careful practice of the processes described in Chapters 3 and 5 and the use of high-quality lapidary machines and supplies.

Jewelry adhesive Adhesive used to attach cabochons to bezels, ring and bracelet blanks, and post-earring bases. A good adhesive is flexible, waterproof, and durable and has moderately fast (but not too fast) drying times. E6000 is a high-quality jewelry adhesive that doesn't need to be mixed. The strongest types of adhesive are two-part epoxy resins that need to be mixed.

Jewelry finding A small metallic implement used to attach a gemstone pendant (such as a cabochon) to a chain or cord. Examples include jump rings, glue-on bails, pinch bails, earring hooks with jump rings, bezels, and ring bases.

Jump ring A small metal ring that attaches to a jewelry finding on a gemstone pendant. A necklace chain or cord is then threaded through the jump ring.

Lapidary A term used to describe a variety of processes, such as cutting, polishing, shaping, and drilling gemstone materials for display or jewelry.

Lapidary grade Stones that are worth the effort and cost to produce beautifully polished pieces for jewelry or display because of the quality of their color and pattern.

Lubricant Used to reduce heat and friction and to capture rock-dust particles such as silica when grinding, sanding, and polishing. The most common lubricant is simple tap water. Others include low-viscosity mineral oils and mixtures with oil additives.

Matte finish A simulated natural finish with a smooth, even surface and a flat, nonglossy texture and appearance.

Mohs hardness scale A scale used to measure the relative hardness of gems and minerals, with 10 being the hardest (diamond), and 1 being the softest (talc). Most of the gemstones used in lapidary processes have a hardness of 6–7.

Natural-shape pendants A thin slice of a whole gemstone that is polished and used for jewelry making. Smaller agates are the primary type of gemstones used for this purpose.

Rapid rinsing A subprocess within the cleanup step for vibratory tumblers. Because vibratory tumblers are top loading, it's easy to pour water and a small amount of liquid soap into the tumbler and then run it for a short time to help remove tumbling grit and polishing compound.

Ring or bracelet base blank A ring or bracelet made to hold a fitted cabochon. Jewelers' adhesive is used to attach the cabochon to the blank.

Rockhound oil/lapidary lubricant A specially formulated mineral oil used for some lapidary saws to cool the blade, reduce the amount of rock dust that could be inhaled, and keep stones from being excessively scratched and fractured while sawing.

Rock tumbler See *rotary tumbler* and *vibratory tumbler.*

Rotary tumbler A lapidary machine used for tumble-polishing stones. The tumbler barrel lies horizontally on the base of the machine and gently tumbles the contents to gradually smooth and polish the gemstone materials.

Rotary hand tool A multipurpose tool that can be used to cut, shape, sand, polish, or drill stone or wood materials. It is best suited to smaller tasks like carving, shaping, and polishing rather than larger tasks like trim-cutting gemstone slabs and making cabochons.

Rough-cutting Cutting away excess material from gemstones for face-polishing or cutting gemstones into slabs.

Semigloss finish Sanding and prepolishing of stones so that they have a luster between glossy and flat.

Silicosis A serious health condition that results from inhaling excessive amounts of rock dust. You can nearly eliminate the risk of silicosis by using lubricants when cutting and grinding and by keeping a ventilation fan running in your work area. You should also wear an N95 or KN95 face mask or respirator.

Sintered Sintered lapidary saw blades feature a narrow strip of crushed diamond particles that are bonded to the blade. This narrow strip does all the cutting work.

Slab saw A saw that's large and powerful enough to cut large whole rocks and rock chunks into slabs. In general, the blade is 10 inches or greater in diameter and the motor is a continuous-duty motor.

Slabbing Cutting gemstone material into thin slices. These slices might be from whole or natural-shape stones (such as agates), or they might be from chunks of stone (such as petrified wood or jasper).

Stages (in polishing) For tumbling and face-polishing, there are multiple stages that bring gemstones from rough material to a matte, semigloss, or high-gloss finish. Within each stage there is a set of repeating steps.

Stencil For lapidary purposes, these are thin plastic or metallic sheets with numerous symmetrical shapes (such as oval, circle, or diamond) that are used to mark gemstone slabs for trim-cutting and then grinding and polishing cabochons.

Steps (in polishing) For tumbling and face-polishing, there are sets of repeating steps within the overall stages. Process steps also occur in the other chapters, but the word "steps" takes on this unique meaning in the "Tumbling" and "Cabochon Making and Face-Polishing" chapters.

Top-drilling When a hole is drilled partway into the top of a gemstone so that a headpin or eyepin can be glued into place and then attached to a necklace or bracelet.

Top loading Vibratory tumblers sit upright, so rocks and water can be put directly into the top of the machine. This is especially useful during the cleaning step of each tumbling stage (also see *rapid rinsing*).

Trim saw A term used to describe lapidary saws. This often leads to confusion about whether separate saws are needed for cutting slabs and for making the finer trim cuts needed for cabochon making. Trim saws have less cutting power and usually aren't continuous duty. They can only cut smaller-size rocks (about 1" diameter).

Tumble-polishing Processing gemstone materials through a series of tumbling stages to produce high-gloss, semigloss, or matte gemstones for display and jewelry pieces.

Tumbling abrasive (or grit) A very hard silicon carbide–based compound used in tumbling processes to smooth out rough edges and prepare the surfaces of gemstones for polishing. Successively finer grit meshes are used as you progress through the tumbling stages.

Tumbling media Small pellets (either ceramic or small pieces of gemstone materials) used in tumble-polishing to help carry the abrasives and polishing compounds and buffer the collisions of gemstones.

Vibratory tumbler A type of lapidary machine used for tumble-polishing stones. The tumbler barrel sits upright. The vibrating motion of the barrel causes its contents to gently roll and slide over each other, gradually smoothing and polishing the gemstone materials.

APPENDIX:
LAPIDARY RESOURCES

Throughout the book, we have talked about the value of working with established providers of lapidary equipment, supplies, and gemstone materials. There are hundreds of businesses around the world that offer these services—far too many to include in this book. However, we'd like to leave you with a few that we have worked with directly and have found to be a good starting point for beginners. Additionally, there are numerous Facebook groups (and YouTube channels) that will be invaluable to beginners and experienced hobbyists. Again, we could provide a much longer list of these groups, but we'll provide just a couple for starters. *We heartily encourage you to seek out suppliers that are local to where you live and compile your own list of trusted resources!*

Kingsley North
kingsleynorth.com
Full-service provider of equipment, supplies, and gemstone materials

The Rock Shed
rockshed.com
Full-service provider of equipment, supplies, and gemstone materials

Minnesota Lapidary Supply
lapidarysupplies.com
Full-service provider of equipment, supplies, and gemstone materials

The Gem Shop
thegemshop.com
Full-service provider gemstone materials and a limited selection of lapidary supplies

RockTumbler.com
rocktumbler.com
Full-service provider of equipment, supplies, and gemstone materials

Etsy
etsy.com
Online portal to small businesses that provide gemstone materials and jewelry findings

Rio Grande Jewelry Supply
riogrande.com
Full-service provider of a wide array of jewelry-making tools and supplies

Lapidary Tips & Tricks
facebook.com/groups/774419732663040
Facebook group that provides interactive information, feedback to member questions, and show-and-tell

Rock & Gem Magazine
rockngem.com
National publication covering lapidary and rockhounding topics

Rock Tumbling and Polishing Group
facebook.com/groups/rockandtumble
Facebook group that provides interactive information, feedback to member questions, and show-and-tell

INDEX

Italicized page numbers represent glossary terms.